WEIRD CANADIAN LAWS

Strange, Bizarre, Wacky & Absurd

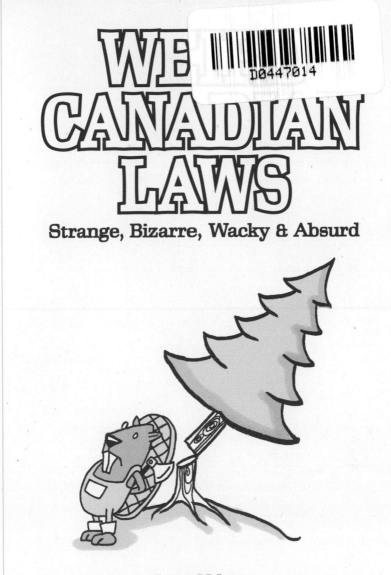

Lisa Wojna

BLUE
BIKE
BOOKS

The Publisher: Blue Bike Books

Library and Archives Canada Cataloguing in Publication

Wojna, Lisa, 1962–
    Weird Canadian laws : strange, bizarre, wacky & absurd / Lisa Wojna;
    Roger Garcia, illustrator.

ISBN-13: 978-1-897278-12-3
ISBN-10: 1-897278-12-8

    1. Law—Canada—Humor. 2. Law—Canada—Popular works.
I. Title.

K184.7.C2W67 2006   349.7102'07   C2006-904511-9

Project Director: Nicholle Carrière
Project Editor: Bridget Stirling
Cover Image: Roger Garcia
Illustrations: Roger Garcia

PC: 1

DEDICATION

To all the new friends I met—through snail mail, e-mail and over the phone—while working on this project. Meeting so many people so willing to help reinforced my belief that ours is the best country in the world.

To Helen and Delilah, who proved the meaning of true friendship a little closer to home.

To my mother, Mary—reading her poems and listening to her play the piano instilled in me a love for all things creative.

And to my dad, Mitch, who always told me to "open my eyes" and "look it up"—two lessons I haven't forgotten.

ACKNOWLEDGEMENTS

Without the kind assistance of a great number of people working at libraries, archives, and city halls across the country, this book simply wouldn't have seen the light of day. Every community mentioned in these pages had a hard-working staff person (with more than enough to keep him or her busy) who gave up a lunch hour or break to pass something of interest my way. Add to that the individuals who agreed to research specific items on my behalf, and I am deeply indebted indeed. My sincerest thanks go out to you all.

I'd like to thank a few people who went beyond all expectations, putting themselves out considerably to help with this project:

☛ Stuart McLean, archivist with the Yarmouth County Museum and Archives in Yarmouth, Nova Scotia. He not only supplied me with laws from his community, but he also dug deep to provide information on some unique laws from his home province as well.

- Edmonton, Alberta's Mayor Stephen Mandel. Many of the blanket e-mails I sent went out to mayors, city clerks, chief administrative officers and other city officials. I decided that if I duplicated my contacts to each community, I'd hopefully hit one person with the time to return my e-mail. I was stunned to have Mayor Mandel personally write me back to tell me he'd passed my request to the appropriate person. Thank you so much for thinking my request important enough for a big city mayor to respond.

- Mayor Jim Sheasgreen of Fort Saskatchewan is another example of the man at the top taking time for what some would see as a troublesome request.

- To Carolina Roemmich of the Prince of Wales Armouries Heritage Centre, City of Edmonton Archives. In record time, she dug up the original versions of a handful of specific repealed laws I'd requested.

- Helen Lowen, librarian with the Law Society Library branch in Wetaskiwin, Alberta. Helen spent hours of her own free time researching items, finding me books, showing me how to use the Canadian Criminal Code and answering countless other questions. Without her invaluable assistance, I would have floundered endlessly in an ocean of legalese.

- As always, to the staff of the Wetaskiwin Public Library.

- Thank you to my editor, Bridget Stirling, and to Nicholle Carrière, the publisher of Blue Bike Books. With so many sections and subsections and overlapping topics, it takes a keen eye to ensure the biggest blooper of all isn't mine!

- And last, but most certainly not least, to my long-suffering family—my husband Garry, children Peter, Melissa, Matthew and Nathan, and my dearest granddaughter Jada. This project has been a particularly time-consuming one, and your support was essential to its completion.

CONTENTS

INTRODUCTION 8

CRIME IN CANADA
No Thanks, We're Canadian 12
Life or Death Matters 14
Fair-market Value 16
Criminal Offensiveness 17
Be Honest, Now 19

BUILDING REGULATIONS
Constructive Behaviour. 21

PAYING THE TAX MAN
Paying Your Dues 24

PROPERTY LAWS
Good Neighbours 27
A Little Respect. 29
Don't Make a Mess!. 30
Greening Up 32

CURFEWS
Do You Know Where Your Children Are?. 35
No Time for Fun. 37

HUNTING REGULATIONS
Tracking Down the Rules 40

THE LORD'S DAY
No-fun Day 43
You Can't Sell That Today! 45

GARBAGE AND GUNK
Outdoor Plumbing. 48
Toilets Go Indoors 52
Take Out the Trash 54

PLANES, TRAINS, AUTOMOBILES AND MORE
Slow Down! 57
Traffic Flow. 61
Snow Messing Around 65
Stop, Thief! 67

Two-wheeled Terrors.................................... 68
Safe Motoring.. 70
Keeping On Track..................................... 71
And Then There Are Some Other Vehicles... 73
It's Not Easy Being Green.............................. 76

GUNS AND AMMO
Ready, Aim, Fire!..................................... 78

YOU CAN'T DO THAT IN PUBLIC
Don't Disturb the Peace 82
You Can't Hang Out There! 84
It's All Fun and Games................................ 85
Keep Your Shirt On 86
Splish Splash... 88

CLEANING UP THOSE ACTS
No Spitting! 90
Clean and Dry 92

BUSINESS ETIQUETTE
That's Show Business! 94
Driving the Rules Home................................ 96
False Advertising..................................... 98
Undercover Sales..................................... 99
Selling in the Streets 101
Food and Drink 103
Who, Where, When? 107
Dining Out... 110
Dirty Business...................................... 112

MIND YOUR MANNERS
Watch Your Mouth 115
Maintaining Morality 116
Ask Nicely.. 119
All Wet 121
Decency Laws 122
And More Good Manners.............................. 123

KEEPING CRITTERS HAPPY
Horsing Around 126
Lively Livestock..................................... 128

Fines for Swine 133
These Laws are for the Birds 134
Domestic and Not-so-domestic Pets 137
Wild Kingdom 142

RULES OF EMPLOYMENT
Earning an Honest Dollar................................. 144

ODDS AND ENDS
Election Time 147
Canadian, By the Rules................................... 148
A Little Respect... 149
Neat and Tidy... 150
An Orderly Fashion...................................... 153
Hot Button Issues 156
Shhh!... 157
Eat, Drink, and Be Legislated 158
Think Globally, Act Locally.............................. 159
Cause for a Celebration.................................. 161
Environment Friendly.................................... 163
Wild Times.. 165
Lock 'Em Up 166
Underwater.. 167

FACT OR FICTION
But Is It a Law?... 169

DEFINITELY LAW
The Law That Wasn't..................................... 175

NO SUCH LAW...NOT YET
Spicing Things Up...At Least Once a Year 177
Water, Water, Everywhere 178
Where There's Smoke... 179
The Public Eye 181

INTRODUCTION

Odd, unique, unusual, and just plain strange—but not necessarily unnecessary. At every level of government, one fact that came across loud and clear as I was researching this collection of interesting laws was that something as simple (yet as complicated) as common sense sometimes needs to be legislated. Behind many of the laws in this collection are some gems of tales. After all, who would have thought Yellowknife city council would have to pass a bylaw prohibiting residents there from owning a pet lion? Yup, there's a whopper of a story behind that one.

Most of the laws in this collection made sense in their day. Likely, they were instituted because someone somewhere did something so out of the ordinary that prosecuting him or her was more difficult than it would have been had a law against the action in question been in place. In other circumstances, bylaws were passed to ensure peace and order for communities and their residents. Still other situations saw laws developed to protect society as a whole—from disease, for example. Hence the "no spitting on public property" bylaws.

Whether they were able to provide an item for this collection or not, most communities I was successful in contacting acknowledged they'd had a strange law—or at least a law that was unique to that community—in their history. Some communities, on the other hand, responded to my request for information by saying they'd never had a strange law on the books, at the present time or in the past. In an email message, Special Constable Rob Ridley of Carstairs, Alberta, explained that the community where he serves was: "Established on May 15, 1903 and recorded in the North-West Territories Gazette on Monday, June 15, 1903, as Order in Council 176/03. Since that time we have attracted such outstanding local governance that no odd or strange law has ever been passed here. Perhaps that is, in itself, unique."

Hmmm. Reflecting a little more on human nature being what it is, nothing strange is very strange indeed!

Then again, another contributor pointed out that what makes sense today may not make sense tomorrow. Ronald M. Swiddle, solicitor for the city of Sudbury, Ontario, said in his written correspondence: "Although we may be accused of having many odd laws now, I am certain that they are not as odd as they will appear in the future. It is the passage of time that makes us realize items that were major concerns in the past. Indeed, there was a time when most rooms contained a spittoon. There was a time when smoking was permitted everywhere. I am certain other of our current activities will seem equally odd through the future's mirror."

Debrah A. Rabbitts, assistant to the mayor and council of the city of Orillia, Ontario, had this anonymous quote attached to the bottom of her email: "Most good judgment comes from experience...most experience comes from bad judgment." It's an apt phrase for the contents of this book.

Some correspondents shared other interesting tidbits from days gone by. For example, J. Harry Beuker, municipal law enforcement officer for the town of Innisfail, Alberta, added this morsel of information. He noted that in the early 1900s, the town's only constable earned $320 per year, plus 10 percent of revenue collected from fines issued. It's hard to imagine that being a sufficient wage to raise a family.

The town of Wilkie, Saskatchewan, contributed this 1922 bylaw setting the town's water rates that, more than pointing to what people could and couldn't do in that community, provides a snapshot of the economics of the day:

- hotels, schools, livery and dray barns: $6.00 per month
- restaurants, laundries, and apartment blocks: $5.00 per month
- dwellings and all other buildings (except the creamery): $3.00 per month

☛ all householders using public connections: $1.00 per month

The communities in this book often change status from one entry to another. I've chosen to refer to them with the status they had at the time they enacted the particular law being mentioned.

Unless otherwise noted and with the exception of the Canadian Criminal Code violations listed, many of the laws in this collection have been repealed.

Sections of the laws that are in quotations are portions taken directly from a law. In these cases, the wording has been kept, either because it adds to the unique flavour of the law or, in some cases, because it is so convoluted as to make the rule unclear altogether.

Most importantly, I'm eternally grateful for the vast amount of information I received from communities across this wonderful country we call home. To know that many busy people took time out of their day to come up with a selection or two for this book is humbling indeed.

It's important to note that while the majority of the information contained in this book was found in primary sources, such as the laws themselves, the snippets entered here are simplified portions of those laws and not a detailed legal assessment. Any error in the interpretation of these laws is entirely mine.

So with all that in mind, kick off your shoes, lean back, and get ready for a good chuckle at the expense of your forefathers. And do so without an ounce of guilt. After all, chances are the youngsters of tomorrow will have a good laugh looking back on the choices we've made today.

Crime
in Canada

From "serious wrong doings" to actions that are
"deemed injurious to the public welfare," committing
a crime in Canada can mean anything from melting
money to murder.

While committing a crime is never funny, there are
some odd situations provided for in the Canadian
Criminal Code.

NO THANKS, WE'RE CANADIAN

Television Regulations

It makes perfect sense that the Canadian Broadcasting Corporation's mandate is to pack its primary viewing hours, from 6:00 AM to midnight, with a minimum of 60 percent Canadian content. But it might surprise you to know that privately owned television stations and networks in Canada face similar requirements. They, too, must meet 60 percent Canadian content requirements from 6:00 AM to midnight, and 50 percent of the airtime between 6:00 PM and midnight must be similarly padded with Canadian-based entertainment.

Radio Regulations

Laws about what can or can not be broadcast on Canadian radio and television because of censorship issues don't appear nearly as stringent as rules about Canadian content. Federal laws stipulate Canadian radio stations must maintain a minimum of 35 percent Canadian content when it comes to weekly music selections. Although their quota is much smaller, ethnic radio stations aren't completely exempt from Canadian content rules either. They must ensure that at least seven percent of the music they air weekly is of Canadian origin.

Their French language counterparts, on the other hand, follow a slightly different set of rules, with a minimum of 65 percent of their weekly music selections required to be in French.

LIFE OR DEATH MATTERS

Prohibiting Provocation

Take 10 paces, turn and shoot. You might be unlucky enough to drop dead, but chances are the guy who shot you might wish he could switch places. That's because inciting someone to fight is against the law in Canada, punishable by two years in prison.

All Murders Are not Created Equal

Shoot to kill and you might still escape incarceration, especially if you feared for your life. According to the Canadian Criminal Code, an individual "made to commit a crime under duress or fear for their safety" is forgiven for his or her actions.

Scared to Death

Technically, you're not in trouble if you frighten someone to death. There is, of course, an exception to every rule. In this case, if you frighten a sick person or a child and they die, you've committed "culpable homicide" and can face criminal charges.

FAIR-MARKET VALUE

And the Winner Is?

By Canadian law, if you enter your name in a free draw, you must still earn what you've just won. No easy come here. Nope, if you want to take home that backyard barbecue you just had your name pulled for, you'd better hope you've read the fine print. Chances are, there was a mathematical question somewhere on the entry form near where you filled out your name and telephone number. Often these questions are simple enough that an elementary school student could answer them, but they need to be answered nonetheless. It appears that it's the idea of getting something for nothing that the Canadian government has a problem with, not the mathematical ability of its residents. Some retailers are more forgiving than the federal government when it comes to giving away free stuff. To help their customers along, they often provide an answer to the "skill-testing question" on the draw box for all to see.

The Value of Money

It's an old trick played by many a youngster—place a penny on a railway track and watch it transform into a flattened piece of copper after a train passes by. But should the proper authorities catch you doing it, the stunt could cost you a $250 fine or a year in jail. That's because in Canada, it is against the law to "melt down, break up or use otherwise than as currency any coin that is current and legal tender in Canada."

CRIMINAL OFFENSIVENESS

That's No Bull!

Livestock can be quite the challenge in Canada. For example, if your prize bull gets it in his head to escape from his pen and wander about, you're likely to face a $25 fine should the right person notice. Now, if that bull decides to have his way with the neighbour's purebred herd and manages to impregnate any (or all) of the cows, you could find yourself in even deeper trouble. Your neighbour could fine you for any and all damages—and keep the resulting offspring as well.

Stinky?

It is against the Canadian Criminal Code for anyone to cause a stink in public—literally. Section 178 of the Criminal Code "makes it a summary conviction offense to do certain things with an offensive volatile substance or a stink or stench bomb."

Sacred Servant

Nothing other than divine intervention can obstruct or prevent a clergy person from conducting a service or performing any other clerical duty. Break the law, and you're guilty of an "indictable offence," and you could face up to two years in jail.

That's Not Funny

Caped crusaders beware! You might soon find yourselves out of work, because it's a breach of the Canadian Criminal Code for illegal acts to be depicted in comic books. As defined in Section C-46 of the 2005 Canadian Criminal Code, a "crime comic" is a picture or image showing the "commission of crimes, real or fictitious" or "events connected with the commission of crimes, real or fictitious, whether occurring before or after the commission of the crime." I'll bet that's news to the creators of Superman!

BE HONEST, NOW

What's In a Name?

It's been said that imitation is the greatest form of flattery. But if you think the Canadian government will be thrilled to learn you've used the words "Parliament Hill" to name your business or to identify the items you sell, you're sadly mistaken. Using "Parliament Hill" to describe anything other than the official site in Ottawa, Ontario, is against the law.

No Fooling

Anyone who fraudulently "pretends to exercise or to use any kind of witchcraft, sorcery, enchantment or conjuration," or claims to tell fortunes or have other paranormal abilities, is guilty of "pretending to practice witchcraft." As with many laws, an intensely obvious question remains. How do you go about discerning whether someone is guilty of pretending or if he or she is, indeed, a gifted psychic?

Truth or Dare

Tell a tale you know is false and have it end up in the pages of your local paper, and you could be charged with spreading false news. If you're guilty, you could face up to two years in jail.

No Questions Asked

Use the words above when advertising a reward for the return of a lost item, and you're guilty of breaking a federal law.

Simply Treasonous!

You'd better practise your manners before taking in a royal visit. That's because it is a crime to startle the Queen in any way. Should you commit the dirty deed, you could spend up to 14 years in jail. Knowingly selling her or any of her representatives defective merchandise is another no-no. The same penalty applies.

Building Regulations

Building regulations were most likely initially enforced for citizens' safety.

While some of the following entries seem like nothing more than common sense, and it boggles the mind how enacting a law was necessary, still others remind us of a time and place long forgotten.

CONSTRUCTIVE BEHAVIOUR

Moving Along

In 1897, if you planned on moving a house in Summerside, PEI, and you had to take a break for a while, you'd better make sure you assigned someone watchman duty. It was against the law to have any "house or building so being removed stand on any street or square without a watchman being in attendance."

Strictly Forbidden

Mud huts and homes with straw roofs were banned in the town of Ponoka, Alberta, in 1914. In the name of fire prevention, residents had to avoid the use of manure, hay, straw and any other "inflammable materials" in the construction of their homes. It appears, however, that wood was not considered an inflammable material.

NO MUD HUTS

Building Code

While the use of coal for heating is nearly obsolete, and there are few trucks delivering coal these days, the city of Sault Ste. Marie, Ontario, still has a regulation on the books regarding the construction of coal chutes. Any business constructing a coal chute is required to submit a detailed drawing to the city engineer. The homeowner must also

- ☞ pay for the construction,
- ☞ pay the city any taxes, and an annual area rental, resulting from the existence of the chute,
- ☞ keep everything in good repair,
- ☞ maintain neighbouring sidewalks and repair any damages resulting from the construction of and delivery of coal,
- ☞ allow the city access, should they require it, for the installation of "pipes, cables, wires, poles and other appliances in or through" the area of the chute" and
- ☞ last, but not least, not even think about holding the city liable should a burglar enter the premises through the coal chute.

Building Permit Required

It cost real estate moguls 50 cents for a building permit in the town of Wilkie, Saskatchewan, in 1913. Failure to comply with this bylaw before building your dream home could cost you $25 or 30 days in jail. The law was repealed in 1923.

Icy Stakes

Cutting ice on lakes, ponds and rivers around Yarmouth, Nova Scotia, was no simple matter in 1916. Town bylaws of that day required anyone cutting ice for home use to identify the area by floating softwood pieces of 4 feet (1.2 metres) or more in length and 3 inches (7.5 centimetres) in diameter. That way (it was hoped), anyone passing by would see the hole in the ice and therefore be protected from an unexpected fall into the frigid waters. Noncompliance, as well as removing stakes from the water, could land you a $20 fine or up to three months in jail.

Paying the Tax Man

It has long been said that the only two guarantees in life are death and taxes, but developing a personal income tax system in Canada was a long, arduous and somewhat unstructured process. Some communities in the country initiated a type of personal income tax system of their own, but they seemed to tax only men of a certain age.

In 1917, the federal government first imposed an annual tax on both people and corporations under the Income War Tax Act. In all provinces except Québec, the federal government took the responsibility for collecting personal taxes away from the municipalities. They also collected corporate taxes for most of Canada, with the exception of Québec, Alberta and Ontario. Of course, the municipalities wouldn't be robbed of their due—they just started collecting taxes of a different sort.

PAYING YOUR DUES

Warfage of Vessels

In 1897, the town of Summerside, PEI, not only charged vessels a parking fee of sorts for docking in their bay, but they also charged a tax on the goods on board. A bylaw dated that year enabled the wharfinger (the keeper of the wharf) the ability to "ask, demand, take and receive of" fees as outlined by the town. For example, ships landing with cedar posts were charged 15 cents per 100 posts. Coal brought in 5 cents a ton and cordwood brought 16 cents a cord. Transported goods not included in the list were charged at a rate of "2 cents per barrel, bulk of 5 cubic feet, or 10 cents per ton, at option of wharfinger."

Tax Time

Businesses, income earners, landowners and "special franchises" in the town of Daysland, Alberta, were first faced with paying municipal and school taxes in 1908. Men aged 21 and older who didn't fit into any of the aforementioned tax categories wouldn't get off scot-free. They had to pay an annual $2.00 poll tax.

A similar poll tax was instituted in the village of Terrace, BC, in 1928. Every male was expected to pay a $5.00 annual tax. The money was used to help support local hospitals and schools.

Work and Taxes

Men aged 21 to 60 living in the town of Cochrane, Alberta, in 1914 were out-of-pocket after the town council passed a bylaw requiring them to pay a $1.00 labour tax, due on May 1 each year. The police chief was responsible for collecting the tax and was authorized to "use all necessary means" to do so.

Income Tax

As of 1925, if you lived in Sault Ste. Marie, Ontario, and earned any money at all, you were required to file a statement of income by May of each year, have your income assessed and possibly pay a tax. Since municipalities no longer have the authority to collect an income tax, the law is no longer in effect.

Property
Laws

Private property doesn't mean you can do whatever you want on your land. There are countless building bylaws regulating what you can and can not do with and on your property in every municipality across the country.

And, of course, what the general public can and can't do on public land is just as restricted. As always, there are rules and regulations for everything.

GOOD NEIGHBOURS

Mend Your Fences

If your dog wandered into the neighbour's wheat field, trampling his way through to the watering hole on the other side, you might have been let off with just a slap on the wrist in 1898. At that time, the law in the North-West Territories, which took up most of Canada west of Neepawa, Manitoba, stated if your property wasn't completely surrounded by a "lawful fence," then the problem was all yours. What constituted a lawful fence varied depending on exactly where you lived. Some areas required a height of 4'6" (1.4 metres), while others required barbed or plain wire secured to posts. So if you wanted to protect yourself, you'd have to be sure of your legal location and the applicable fencing requirements.

Measure Up!

Fences are strictly regulated in London, Ontario. If your neighbour builds a fence, it can't be less than 3'6" (1.07 metres) or more than 4'6" (1.37 metres) in height. And barbed wire is absolutely forbidden within city limits.

Dim Those Lights!

A front yard light might make you feel safe at night, but if its glow flows beyond your property line, you could find yourself face to face with a bylaw officer. That's the law in the city of Regina, Saskatchewan.

Pristine Property

Property owners in the town of Morden, Manitoba, are expected to follow strict guidelines when it comes to upkeep. Along with the obvious expectations of cleanliness and safety, the town council restricts the number of vehicles parked or stored on a person's land, and it's against a 2001 bylaw for residents to store household appliances in a location "visible from any public street, road or lane." The town also monitors excessive weed growth and unkempt lawns. So if your dandelions are growing out of control, you'd better get your weed whacker out. Breaking any portion of the bylaw could result in town workers taking the matters into their own hands—and charging you for it!

Hot and Cold

Air conditioners and heat exchangers must be strategically placed in Regina homes. A bylaw in that Saskatchewan city states they can't be "closer to the front lot line than the front wall" of the building they are attached to and "closer than 3 metres (10 feet) to a door or window of a dwelling on an adjoining lot."

A LITTLE RESPECT

Looking After Our Elders

The city of Whitehorse, Yukon, takes the responsibility of caring for its elders seriously. In an effort to compensate for seniors' growing utility bills, a 2002 bylaw gives everyone aged 65 and older an annual grant of up to $500.

A Grave Situation

It's been said you know the quality of a society by the way they treat their dead. And it seems to be an apt adage for the people of Bowden, Alberta. In 1954, the village council enacted a bylaw outlining specific regulations for cemeteries. In particular, they went to great lengths to explain how excess earth is to be removed from the site immediately after the grave is filled in. They then required that "gravel, stone, paper or boxes or anything of a similar nature...be removed within 48 hours after the burial," even being so particular as to rule that "nothing of a size greater than one square inch be left in the vicinity of the grave."

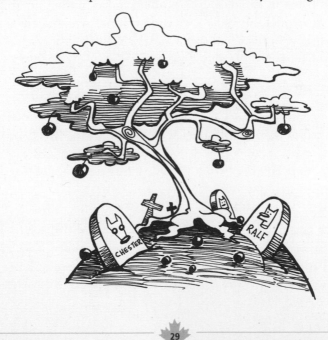

DON'T MAKE A MESS!

Art, No Art

City officials in Regina, Saskatchewan, don't look kindly on graffiti. Though some would beg to differ, in that city, it's not art—it's a crime. To put an end to vandalism, city officials passed a bylaw providing residents with some hints on how to combat the problem. They suggest property owners

- grow plants along the exterior walls of buildings,
- use "anti-graffiti coatings on surfaces previously covered by graffiti" or
- pay artists to paint murals on areas attracting graffiti.

The image that comes to mind, should everyone follow these rules to the letter, is an aerial view of nothing but greenery and an occasional mural.

Snow Littering

An old bylaw in Parkdale, PEI, prohibited people from littering town streets and sidewalks—with snow! It was one of many outdated bylaws in the Charlottetown Area Municipalities Act repealed between 1997 and 2002.

Trim Those Trees

Out-of-control greenery encroaching on town sidewalks or on public roadways is against the law in Oak Bay, BC. In 1994, council made it law for residents to control their foliage with a Hazardous Tree and Shrub Bylaw.

Safety Conscious

For the sake of public safety, in 1914, the town of Ponoka, Alberta, enacted a lengthy bylaw restricting a number of potentially dangerous behaviours. You couldn't break, train or breed your horse in town. You couldn't fasten your horse to any "tree, shrub or sapling." Sidewalks were made for people, not for bikes, horses or carriages. Even wheelbarrows and tricycles were forbidden on town sidewalks. It was illegal to use barbed wire when building a fence that bordered any highway, street, road lane, alley or byway in town limits. In fact, any errant nail protruding through the fence post could get you into trouble as well.

And business owners weren't allowed to sweep their way out their store doors and onto town sidewalks. They were expected to collect their rubbish in a dustpan and dispose of it in a properly enclosed garbage can.

Nothing but a Nuisance

A bylaw passed by the city of Kelowna, BC, in 1932 made it illegal to "excavate a hole or pit on any property by removing soil, sand or gravel unless erecting a building." The reason was simple—holes and pits were a nuisance. The penalty for breaking this bylaw was $100, and it wasn't repealed until 1990.

GREENING UP

Saving Water

The laws of supply and demand are strictly adhered to in the city of Guelph, Ontario. So much so that in 2003, the city council enacted a bylaw stating it was against the law to water your lawn during a rainstorm. Allowing tap water to pool around plants and trees or to run off you lawn and onto the street in front of your home also could be cause for a visit from the city's bylaw officer. The same bylaw states that hosing down your driveway rather than sweeping up any dry dirt or debris is another no-no. Break the law, and the city could decide to reduce the amount of water supplied to your home.

Two Will Do

The town of Cochrane, Alberta, has taken its commitment to environmental consciousness seriously after the council in that community passed a new waste management bylaw in December 2005. In Cochrane, it doesn't matter if you have a family of two or twelve. Residents now have a "two unit limit" when it comes to having their garbage picked up at the curb. And what constitutes a single unit is not just any size of garbage bag. A bag larger than 66 by 91 centimetres is now treated as two units— no exceptions! If, on special occasions, you have an extra bag to add to your curbside pickup, that garbage must be placed in a special "Town of Cochrane Excess Waste Bag" for an additional $2.00 fee.

Collection of Compost

The town council in Stavely, Alberta, may have yet to pass a bylaw on the matter, but they have distributed a notice to all town residents explaining how compost garbage "must be bagged in clear bags." The council-sanctioned bags can be purchased at the Stavely Grocery Store and, for residents choosing this option, the compost drop-off is only open on Fridays from 8:00 AM to 3:00 PM.

Curfews

"What can't you do during the day that you have to be out of doors after dark?" Many of us can recall having one parent or another ask this question at some point during our youth. And it appears youngsters staying outside after dark were of concern to the general population throughout the ages.

Although curfew laws are still on the books in several communities, and rumblings about enacting curfew bylaws in towns and cities across the country are a topic of frequent news reports, this kind of bylaw is rarely enforced.

DO YOU KNOW WHERE YOUR CHILDREN ARE?

Curfew Bell

In 1895, the Women's Christian Temperance Union played its part when it came to regulating the whereabouts of youngsters in the town of Dresden, Ontario. The ladies did this by ringing the town bell daily at 9:00 PM to remind residents it was curfew time. The bell was the signal for all youths age 16 and younger to be off public streets and in their homes or suffer the wrath of the on-duty constable. If youngsters weren't safe in the loving arms of their families after the curfew bell sounded, they would get a free ride, courtesy of the constable, and their parents or guardians could be fined as much as $5.00. The fine increased depending on the frequency of the youngster's rebellion.

Curfew Time

In Sault Ste. Marie, Ontario, a curfew for youth 16 and under was established by enacting a bylaw "in accordance with the provisions of the Children's Protection Act of Ontario." Parents or guardians permitting their youngsters to wander the streets after

9:00 PM would be fined $1.00 for a first offence and $2.00 for a second offence. Break the law three or more times, and they were fined $5.00 each time. While this bylaw was passed in 1921 and is still on the books, it hasn't been enforced, since according to city officials, it wouldn't likely survive a Canadian Charter of Rights and Freedoms challenge based on age discrimination.

Still the Law

A currently active curfew bylaw in Churchill, Manitoba, provides youth there with a stepping-stone of sorts to obtaining the rights of adulthood. Youth aged 11 and younger have to be off the streets and at home by 10:00 PM. Youth 12 to 16 have an extra hour before they're in trouble for roaming about unaccompanied by a parent, and youth over 16 but not yet the "age of majority," (which in Manitoba is 18) have to be safe and sound behind closed doors by midnight. This curfew bylaw also applies to being in a "public place" without a parent or adult guardian.

Police escort young lawbreakers home. If there is no adult available to meet the officer escort, and one can't be found in short order, the teen could find him or herself "delivered to the appropriate child care agency."

Churchill has a rather unique way of doling out punishment to fit this crime as well. For youth involved, a first offence warrants a warning, and any second and subsequent offense will cost as much as $100 and assigned community service hours.

Parents and guardians who don't take the curfew laws seriously could find themselves back in school: "Any guardian that is found in contravention of this bylaw a second time shall be sent to community services to receive parenting classes."

NO TIME FOR FUN

Dance With Me

You may like to swing your partner 'round and 'round the dance floor, but there were strict guidelines on how far into the wee hours you could party in the village of Smithers, BC, in 1934. The council enacted a curfew bylaw of a unique sort, stating that the last tune played at any dance had to end by midnight on Saturday and by 2:00 AM on any other night of the week. It seems the reasoning behind this was to ensure partiers had a relatively early night on Saturday, giving them no excuses for not filling the pews at Sunday morning worship.

Early to Bed

In 1947, the village of Smithers, BC, agreed to amend their curfew bylaw of 1930. The original curfew mandated that children age 15 and younger had to be indoors by 9:00 PM during the winter months of October to March and by 10:00 PM from April to September. The court could fine people who allowed their youngsters out past curfew unaccompanied by a parent or guardian. But the situation caused a whole lot of problems for peace officers on days the "Moving Picture Theatre of the Village of Smithers" was operating, since the movies didn't typically end until 10:00 PM or later. To accommodate the situation and keep parents and their youngsters happy—not to mention the owner of the movie theatre and the peace officers on duty those nights—village council agreed to extend the curfew, on movie nights only, to 10:30 PM.

Hunting
Regulations

Hunters beware!

While you might think you have the corner on the market when it comes to knowing all there is to know about hunting, think again. We may all be Canadian, but hunting regulations differ from province to province and are continually evolving throughout.

See what I mean…

TRACKING DOWN THE RULES

Laws of Yesteryear

In 1909, Alberta's Minister of Agriculture paid a bounty of $10 for each timber wolf pelt, $1.00 for each prairie wolf pelt and $1.00 for each wolf pup pelt. But if the wolves you claimed that you killed in Alberta actually came from outside the province, you could face a $100 fine.

Laws of Today

☛ Animals may pose a nuisance as they wander through town streets, but you still can't hunt or trap wild prey in Canmore, Alberta. A 1991 bylaw makes it clear, stating that a hunter could be fined as much as $2500 for his efforts.

☛ It is against the law to use a pistol, revolver or "any firearm that is capable of firing more than one bullet during one pressure of the trigger" while hunting in Alberta.

☛ Hunters going after big game in Saskatchewan must be completely outfitted with an "outer suit of scarlet, bright yellow, blaze orange or white or any combination of these colors." Head gear of one of these colours, except white, must also be worn.

☛ Brightly coloured clothing is not required for hunters in Alberta. The only exception to this rule is for those hunting on Camp Wainwright, but bow hunters hunting in the bow-only portion of Camp Wainwright are exempt from clothing rules.

The Lord's Day

From the founding of this country until well into the 20th century, Sunday was considered a sacred day of rest. All but the most essential services stopped for this 24-hour period, and people were expected to do just that—rest.

But what form that "rest" took was almost as controversial as later decisions to open retail businesses and liquor stores on Sundays.

NO-FUN DAY

Batter Up!

Throughout most of Canada's early history, keeping the Lord's Day holy meant regulating what events could and could not occur on Sunday. But in 1968, the town of Blenheim, Ontario, did bend the rules slightly. They decided that public sports, previously banned on the day of rest, could be played after 1:30 PM. And they were very specific as to which sports would get the reprieve. Approved athletic activities included "baseball, softball, fast ball, football, rugby, rugger, soccer, hockey, lacrosse, tennis, badminton, swimming and aquatic sports events, tract [track] and field, bowling and curling, public skating and figure skating."

The town of Cochrane, Alberta, was a step ahead of Blenheim, having passed a similar law in 1950. Cochrane, too, listed those sports allowed, and the town's list, for the most part, mirrored Blenheim's. Looks like if you played basketball, volleyball or ping pong, you were out of luck—at least in these two communities.

Let the Show Begin!

Laws surrounding Sunday activities loosened slightly in 1967 in the town of Trenton, Ontario, after a referendum of sorts was held and the majority of the public agreed that a little entertainment on Sunday afternoons wasn't any great sin. The council members of the day agreed, and on January 15, 1968, it was deemed lawful for movies, theatrical performances, concerts and lectures to be held after 1:30 PM.

Clean Fun Only

While restrictions on participating in or attending events such as air and car shows or taking part in certain sporting events on Sundays were loosened in the town of Fahler, Alberta, in 1968, some activities were still taboo. It was still against the law to engage in or attend "horse races, or horse race meetings, dog races, boxing contests or exhibitions of wrestling or other like contests or exhibitions" on Sundays.

Still Revered

The year is 2002. The Yukon has revised its statutes, and the Lord's Day Act is still on the books. Residents there can take part in sporting events and other recreational activities, provided the event begins after 1:30 PM. Sunday movies, concerts and other performances are okay as well, as long as they also follow the time stipulation. There is a provision to repeal the statute, but it would take a vote by the electorate saying they are "in favour of the repeal of the bylaw passed under the authority of the Lord's Day Act that regulates public games and sports for gain after 1:30 o'clock in the afternoon of the Lord's Day." To date, a public vote has not been held.

YOU CAN'T SELL THAT TODAY!

Got Gas?

If you ran out of gas on a Sunday in the village of Fahler, Alberta, in 1954, you couldn't fill up at just any gas station. The village passed a bylaw stating that all but one gas station in the community had to remain closed on Sunday. Each gas station would take a turn at being the lucky station open each week, and all other stations were responsible for posting a notice in a prominent place directing needy customers to the open station. Any gas station owner opening for business on a Sunday when it wasn't his or her turn would have the station closed by the village constable. The fine for a first offence was $5, $25 for the second offence and as much as $100 for a third or subsequent offence.

Open for Business

Depending on the type of wares they pedalled, shop owners in the village of Smithers, BC, had to abide by strict "Lord's Day" guidelines as early as 1934. Other than "Automobile Repair Shops or Gasoline Service Stations," all shops were to be closed on Sundays and all statutory holidays. Regular shop hours of 8:45 AM to 6:00 PM were kept from Monday to Wednesday and on Friday. Thursday, however, was subject to the "Weekly Half Holiday Act," and closing time was moved back to 1:00 PM. Shop owners were allowed to compensate for some of the closed hours on Thursday by staying open to 9:00 PM on Saturday. And just because you might be selling your goods as a street vendor instead of an actual store, the law still applied. "Hawkers and Peddlers" weren't allowed to sell goods when stores were closed. The fine for breaking any portion of this bylaw could cost you $100—a pretty penny in the Dirty Thirties.

Garbage
and Gunk

*Public sanitation and the health of residents go hand
in hand, and from the earliest days, newly founded communities across the country were quick to formulate laws
in this regard.*

*While all were logical (after a fashion), it seems bizarre
that some needed to be mentioned at all.*

OUTDOOR PLUMBING

The Throne

Construction of an outhouse at every home or public place was mandatory in the town of Ponoka, Alberta, in 1929. And not just any old outhouse would do. A seat must be securely attached to the framework of the outhouse "in such a manner that same may be easily and expeditiously lifted up and left standing open when required." A 5-gallon (19-litre) galvanized bucket was to be used as a receptacle, and any previously dug pit-style outhouse was to be dismantled and covered in. The bucket had to be dumped twice a month in the appropriate corner of the town's nuisance grounds. Refuse to comply with this bylaw, and the town could take it on itself to build your personal throne for you, charge you for materials and labour and then hit you with a fine of up to $50 or 60 days in jail, "with or without hard labour."

Public Record

A sanitary bylaw in Terrace, BC, required the staff person responsible for removing "night soil" to follow a set of stringent guidelines. He had to maintain a record of all toilets in the municipality and provide a monthly report to the village clerk, complete with each owner's name and the dates of cleaning. Talk about airing your dirty laundry in public! Residents interfering with the cleaning of their toilet faced a fine of up to $25.

No-fly Zone

Outhouse regulations were a little less stringent in the village of Quesnel, BC. In 1950, a bylaw regulated the style of an outhouse but still allowed a dugout pit. However, the bylaw did stipulate that this outdoor privy should be "so banked and eased as to be absolutely fly tight."

Keep Your Distance

A 1946 bylaw in the village of Westlock, Alberta, outlined a list of specific distances an outhouse could be located from different buildings. They had to be within 5 feet (1.5 metres) of the rear property line of any lot, at least 2 feet (60 centimetres) from a lane or adjoining lot, a minimum of 50 feet (15 metres) from any well site and at least 20 feet (6 metres) from any "dwelling, store, restaurant or any other place where food is stored or consumed."

Price Per Pail

A 1910 bylaw in the town of Okotoks, Alberta, also required residents to outfit their outhouses with metal pails, rather than just dirt pits. According to Lucy Rowed, historical assistant with the town of Okotoks Museum and Archives, "The 'Scavenger' was duly appointed to empty unmaintained, overflowing or stinky closets at a cost to the owner of 25 cents per pail."

Bucket Brigade

Weyburn, Saskatchewan, was strict about the disposal of the contents of the family waste bucket. In 1913, the town enacted a bylaw outlining all the particulars of waste management in that community. First, residents not connected with the city sewer system were required to purchase (at cost) a specially regulated "galvanized iron pail" measuring about 2 ft^2 (0.05 m^3). The homeowner was then expected to build an outhouse of sorts, following specific regulations outlined by the city, to house the pail.

Pail Provided

In Wilkie, Saskatchewan, the sanitation system for personal waste was subject to yet another set of unique regulations. In a 1930 town bylaw, the council legislated that every homeowner had to provide an "outside pail closet" that was completely "fly-proof" and had "self-closing covers." No additional garbage of any kind, such as kitchen waste or used wash water, could be added to the contents of closet pails. For the convenience of having town officials dispose of the contents of these pails on a regular basis, each homeowner was charged an annual fee of $8.00 per pail. And not just anyone had the privilege of collecting the contents of these pails. In fact, any unauthorized person removing or disposing of any night soil could face a fine of his or her own.

Water Closet Etiquette

In 1924, the town of Cochrane, Alberta, passed a bylaw making it illegal to plug the town's sewer system by putting "garbage, offal, dead animals, vegetable parings, ashes, cinders, rags, strings, hair combings, matches or any other matter or thing that would tend to obstruct any pipe or sewer in any water closet, bathtub, wash bowl, kitchen sink or any other fixture connected with the sewer system of the town of Cochrane." To ensure no one—residents and their guests alike—broke this law, it was also stipulated that each householder post a complete copy of the bylaw in a clearly visible place in any bathroom or washing area so that no one could use the excuse he or she wasn't aware of the restrictions. Failure to follow the bylaw could cost the offender $50 or up to 21 days in jail—that was, once the jails were finally built!

TOILETS GO INDOORS

Indoor Plumbing

In 1950, indoor washrooms, or water closets, were coming into fashion in the village of Quesnel, BC, necessitating the institution of a bylaw regulating their construction in that community. Should a homeowner install a water closet in his or her dwelling, a window measuring 3 ft^2 (0.9 m^2) and able to open to at least half its height was required.

Bathroom Rules

A 1975 bylaw in the city of Kelowna, BC, states: "every dwelling house, hotel, boarding house, rooming house, restaurant, store, factory and manufactory or whatsoever kind, erected within the city shall have a water-closet, toilet or lavatory accommodation in connection therewith." While the idea seems like a no-brainer, this law is still in effect.

Privy Patrol

When you gotta go, you gotta go—or so the saying goes. But in the town of Barrhead, Alberta, finding a pit stop for the purpose of relieving yourself became a little more difficult after the town council passed a bylaw in 1970 ordering privies removed from some private properties. According to the bylaw, homes on land bordering town streets where sewer and water mains were located had to be connected with town service. Water closets or privies not connected to the town's system had to be removed from the property within 30 days of notice from the town. Failure to do so meant the town could send their people in to do the dirty work and add the cost of the effort to the property owner's taxes.

TAKE OUT THE TRASH

Ashes to Ashes

The disposal of ashes must have posed a significant challenge in years past, since bylaws managing their disposal were enacted in many communities across the country. No one—householder or servant—was allowed to deposit ashes in any street, lane, road or public property of any sort in the town of Lloydminster, Alberta. The 1913 bylaw went on to specify that ashes were to be placed in a metal container not less than 27 inches in height and 3 inches in diameter. They were to remain in the container until cool, but the bylaw doesn't go on to explain where they should be deposited at that point. Still, dare to defy what was written and you could face a $10 fine or 20 days in jail.

Careful With That

Disposing of ashes in the town of Carman, Manitoba, was no simple matter in December 1955. That's when town council passed a law outlining the appropriate manner of getting rid of the potentially flyaway garbage. According to the new bylaw, ashes simply couldn't be dumped in the street or on any town property, and anyone caught dumping ashes would face a $2.00 fine for each offense. Strangely enough, the law was repealed just a few months later.

In the Can

In 1929, Ponoka, Alberta, definitely had a say in how you disposed of your household waste. The town enacted a law that garbage not able to be burned must be placed in a tightly sealed zinc or galvanized "refuse bucket." This garbage can was to be located at the rear of each home and business property, and town employees collected the contents once a week. Homes and businesses not providing a garbage bucket for themselves would be provided with one—and subsequently charged for the item—by the town and could face a $50 fine or up to 60 days in jail for non-compliance.

Planes, Trains,
Automobiles and More

*Keeping people safe on roads, lanes, streets and
highways has been a major concern for communities
everywhere from the days of the first horse-drawn carts.
Developing rules of the road makes good sense. After all,
you can't have traffic moving in all directions without
causing some sort of disaster. Just try driving the wrong
way on a one-way street!*

*What is interesting, however, is how some
communities regulated everything from when and where
you could push your wheelbarrow to common-sense
pedestrian protocol.*

SLOW DOWN!

No Speed Freaks Here

In the town of Peace River, Alberta, anyone driving a vehicle of any description—horse-drawn buggy, automobile or even unicycle—couldn't exceed a speed of 6 miles per hour (9.7 kilometres per hour) "while in the act of crossing over the Harmon River Bridge." Considering that a brisk power walker likely exceeds the 6 mile per hour limit, one is hard-pressed to understand why anyone would bother driving their vehicle into town at all. Still, break the law, and you could face a fine of $100. And if you were unable to pay, you could face a prison sentence of up to 60 days, "with or without hard labour." Also known as Heart River Bridge, the structure was located within town limits. The 1925 bylaw doesn't mention if the same speed was enforced throughout the rest of the town.

Slow-moving Vehicles

Motorized vehicles of any kind were kept restrained in the town of Lloydminster, Alberta, in 1919. That's when the town fathers enacted a speed limit of 12 miles per hour. If you dared to speed through that community, a hefty fine of up to $50 was charged for a first offense. And if you didn't control that heavy foot of yours, second and subsequent fines were double that. If you couldn't pay the piper, you had to pack your bags and spend the next 30 days in jail.

Back Lane Safety

The city of Winnipeg, Manitoba, eliminated one speeding loophole in 1978. Anyone driving down a back lane must keep his speed to a maximum of 30 kilometres per hour. The law was updated in 2002 and is still in effect.

Easy Does It

The town of Okotoks didn't adhere to rushing about, especially when it came to motor vehicle traffic. A 1910 bylaw restricted the speed in town to 10 miles per hour (16 kilometres per hour), and reduced that further to 5 miles per hour (8 kilometres per hour) when approaching another car. An article in the *Okotoks Review* stated: "Every precaution must be taken to avoid accident, even to stopping car altogether."

Tough on Traffic

The town of Wilkie, Saskatchewan, was pretty tough on all types of traffic using town streets and sidewalks in 1922. An extensive bylaw developed that year regulated everything from speed limits to parking. For example, slow traffic, including horses and motor vehicles travelling less than 4 miles per hour (6.5 kilometres per hour), had to hug the curb when travelling through town. Vehicles were considered "fast traffic" when they were travelling more than 4 miles per hour (6.5 kilometres per hour).

Most rules of the road were similar to those of today. What was unique was how horses and Fords were treated alike. Both were expected to pass to the left of slow traffic. When meeting at a stop sign, the horse or motor vehicle to the right had the right of way. However, the bylaw does get a little muddy when referring to parking regulations. For example, it stipulates "No vehicle shall stop with its left to the curb." One would assume this didn't apply to a solitary horse and saddle operation, since it's pretty hard to get a horse to stand still at its tether while you do your shopping!

Pace Yourself

A 1910 amendment to a 1901 bylaw added a few restrictions to the speed of horse travel in the town of Rat Portage (now Kenora), Ontario. Your equine-powered transportation—with or without carriage—couldn't pass across bridges in the town "at any rate of speed greater or faster than a walk."

Whoa, Nellie!

The first cars might not have made their appearance yet on the streets of North Battleford, Saskatchewan, in 1906, but speed limits were still strictly enforced. Horses couldn't gallop, carriage drivers needed to slow down through town and racing of any kind was strictly prohibited. Slow-moving traffic travelling less than 4 miles per hour (6.5 kilometres per hour) had to pull over as close to the right curb as possible to allow other traffic to pass by. And if you decided to stop by the local market and pick up a few things, you'd better make sure your horse was secured to something strong enough to prevent him from getting loose.

In 1917, another traffic bylaw in the same community defined the term "vehicle" as including "equestrians, led horses and everything on wheels or runners, drawn or driven by animal or mechanical power of every description, except baby carriages." In that same bylaw, the word "horse" included "horses, mules, oxen or other beasts of burden."

TRAFFIC FLOW

Keep the Streets Clear

"No person" was allowed to tie his horse or horses to "any ring or hook in any other way across the sidewalk, path or crossing" in the village of Standard, Alberta. The 1923 bylaw prevented the gathering of any group of people as well, so it's safe to say a protest rally of any kind wasn't in the cards.

Well, Duh!

According to a 1965 traffic bylaw in the village of Quesnel, BC, you were absolutely prohibited from building any "structure, object, substance, or thing" in the middle of any street. After all, you could block the flow of traffic!

Don't Play in Traffic

There is a time and place for athletic amusement, and the middle of the street is simply not the right place at any time, according to a 1965 traffic bylaw in Quesnel, BC. Council deemed it against the law to do anything on city streets that might be "likely or calculated to frighten horses or embarrass or delay the passage of vehicles."

Safe Parking
At one time it was against the law to park any closer than 10 feet (3 metres) from a house in Calgary, and that included a car, carriage or wagon.

Safe Streets

Wilkie, Saskatchewan's town council went all out making sure their town streets were safe in 1922. They passed a bylaw making it illegal to throw stones, balls of ice or snow, hard balls of any kind or any other "dangerous missile or use any bow and arrow in the street."

Parking Prohibited
It was against the law in 1922 in the town of Wilkie, Saskatchewan, to park a carriage on town streets and unhitch your horse. While parked on town streets, carriage and horse had to remain as one unit.

City Streets

A bylaw passed in the city of St. John's, Newfoundland, in 1970 made it illegal to dig a hole, ditch, drain or sewer in city streets without first getting a permit from the city engineer.

First-class Delivery
Anyone dropping a package of any kind on the streets or sidewalks of St. John's, Newfoundland, is guilty of obstructing free passage and could face a $25 fine.

Comfortable Passage

Since 1970, sidewalks in the city of St. John's, Newfoundland, have to be a minimum of 3.048 metres wide on streets that are 18.288 metres in width and larger—and yes, the bylaw is that precise! Sidewalk width on narrow streets was to be determined by a meeting of council.

Keep It Moving

The Grand Parade, an area in downtown Halifax, Nova Scotia, holds special significance to the residents of that city. So much so that the council enacted a bylaw in 1950 making it illegal for residents to leave a vehicle standing stationary and abandoned without written permission from the public works department. You also couldn't skateboard in the area. Either offense was punishable by a $20 fine or 10 days in jail.

Foot Traffic

Pedestrians had their rules and regulations drawn out in detail for them after the town of Yarmouth, Nova Scotia, passed a bylaw in 1923. Just like vehicles driving on the road, people on foot had to pass oncoming pedestrians to the right. When passing a person walking in the same direction as yourself, you had to pass them on their left. If you happened to be walking side by side with a friend, you'd have to move to a single-file formation when meeting oncoming pedestrians. And it was absolutely against the law for two or more baby carriages to be wheeled side by side on any sidewalk.

No Parking

In the early 1900s, the town of Innisfail, Alberta, passed a bylaw requiring all horses and horse-powered vehicles be parked on the south side of Main Street. Because Main Street runs east and west in Innisfail, the south side of the street gave some shade to horses on hot summer days.

Clear the Sidewalks

It is illegal to "lead, ride or drive a horse or cattle" on the sidewalks of Digby, Nova Scotia. The "Horses and Cattle Bylaw" was enacted in 1975. Residents insisting on walking their livestock on the sidewalk were slapped with a $100 fine or two months in the nearest jail. This law wasn't repealed until 2000.

SNOW MESSING AROUND

Snow Exceptions

It is against the law to operate a snowmobile within town limits in Morden, Manitoba—unless, of course, a snowstorm has shut down highways to regular vehicle traffic.

Off Limits

The town of Beausejour, Manitoba, accepts snowmobile traffic between October 15 and April 15 as a regular part of life. Snowmobile operators there are expected to "share the roadways with other vehicular traffic." Of course, they're expected to obey all Criminal Code, Highway Traffic Act and off-road regulations. Oh, and one more thing. They are absolutely prohibited from travelling the streets of Park Avenue and First Street North.

Snow Sailing

In 1971, the village of Airdrie, Alberta, passed a bylaw allowing "Ski-Doos to use the east and west lanes" for travel in and out of the community but only between the hours of 10:00 AM and 10:00 PM. The bylaw was repealed in 1982.

Insurance Please

A 1994 bylaw okayed riding a snowmobile in Whitehorse, Yukon. But if the local authorities stop you, you'd better have read the small print. While the use of "motor toboggans" is fine, you must have valid insurance. Every snowmobiler must also have a set of identification numbers "placed upon the hood of his motor, toboggan or some other conspicuous place thereon."

Sleigh Bells Ring!

Even the horse-drawn sleighs of yesteryear had horns—of sorts. To warn pedestrians of their approach, the town of Lloydminster, Alberta, made it law in 1916 that any horse, mule or other animal pulling a sleigh through city streets must be equipped with bells.

STOP, THIEF!

Take Your Keys!

In a concerted effort to reduce auto theft in 1955, the town of Fahler, Alberta, passed a bylaw permitting the town constable to remove the keys from cars parked within town limits during the evening and night. Apparently it was fairly common practice at the time for motorists to leave their doors unlocked and their keys in the ignition. Drivers who'd had their keys confiscated only had to "apply" to the constable to have them returned. This "service" was provided "free of charge."

Lock the Doors

Leaving your car unattended and unlocked wasn't just a potential lure to thieves, it was also against the law in the town of Cochrane, Alberta, in 1948. The rationale behind the rule was to prevent an unauthorized person from jumping in the driver's seat and taking the vehicle for a spin. Unfortunately, if the car was stolen, the owner wasn't just missing his vehicle. Reporting it could cost him as much as $10 or 21 days in jail!

TWO-WHEELED TERRORS

Do You Have a Licence for That Thing?

If you were found riding your bicycle through the streets of Fort Saskatchewan, Alberta, without a licence in 1945, you could find yourself facing a fine. That year, council passed a bylaw making bicycle licences mandatory.

Measure Those Wheels

Westlock, Alberta, enacted a bylaw in 1946 stating that no one could ride a bicycle with wheels larger than 46 centimetres (18 inches) on village sidewalks or boulevards. Smaller wheels appear to have been okay, though.

Don't Lose Control

Riding a bicycle might be good for your health, but let go of those handlebars, and you might find your face planted in a roadside hedge. This could be why the city of Vernon, BC, used a portion of an old bylaw and incorporated it into their current traffic bylaw. Section 805 states: "No rider of a bicycle shall remove both hands from the handle bars or feet from the pedals, or practice any acrobatic or fancy riding on any street." The earlier bylaw contributing this remnant dated back to 1949.

Bicycles Beware

As early as 1916, the village of Lloydminster, Alberta, enacted a bylaw stating bicycles of any size were not allowed on village sidewalks. They had to share the roads with all other vehicle traffic of the day.

Blow That Horn

Bicycles in Wilkie, Saskatchewan, had to have a "proper alarm bell, gong or horn," and bike riders were expected to blow their horn to signal their approach to pedestrians and other road traffic. The same 1922 bylaw also legislated that, similar to other vehicle traffic, bicycles were required to "carry in front...a lighted lamp from one hour after sunset to one hour before sunrise."

SAFE MOTORING

Eyes On the Road

Newfoundland and Labrador leads the country when it comes to legislating cell phone use. As of April 1, 2003, that province made it illegal to "use a handheld cellular phone while driving." A motorist caught talking on the phone while driving can be charged under a "number of provincial, territorial or federal laws including, but not limited to, those related to dangerous driving, careless driving and (in the case of an accident) criminal negligence causing death or injury."

Red Means Stop

It may be clear sailing for miles around, but you still can't turn right on a red light in Québec. Although the law has been repeatedly disputed, it's still in effect.

10 and 2

A 1965 traffic bylaw in the town of Quesnel, BC, made it illegal to drive a car or a bicycle without keeping at least one hand on the steering wheel. Youngsters on bikes, trikes, roller skates or sleighs were forbidden from catching rides by grabbing on to moving vehicles. And it was against the law for the driver of any vehicle to "permit any part of his body or any part of a passenger's body to extend outside the vehicle." The only exception to the rule was when the driver needed to perform a turning signal.

Imagine That?

A law passed in 1918 in the town of Yarmouth, Nova Scotia, made it illegal to drive any type of vehicle the wrong way down a one-way street. The same traffic bylaw made it mandatory for drivers to use signals when stopping or turning. They were to do so by "raising a whip or hand vertically."

KEEPING ON TRACK

Whistling Softly

What was initially seen as a safety measure has fast become an urban nuisance, and for some communities across the country, that nuisance had to be dealt with. The city of Winnipeg, Manitoba, first silenced train whistles going through town in 1979. But the engineer travelling through the city had better stay sharp, since other than the 20 crossings listed in the bylaw where sounding the engine whistle is prohibited, he can blow to his heart's content everywhere else.

Right of Way

In Cornerbrook, Newfoundland, it is illegal to change gears when crossing a railway track. This restriction is part of Newfoundland's Highway Traffic Act of 1990. What's strange about this law is that since the provincial government shut down and disassembled the railroad in the 1980s, there are no longer any trains operating in that province.

More Powerful than a Speeding Locomotive?

Cross a set of railway tracks in front of an oncoming train, and it doesn't matter how large your vehicle is—there's no doubt who will win. Still, the Newfoundland Act of 1892 made it illegal to cause any injury to railway trains. Anyone caught damaging any railway property could be sentenced to a jail term of up to 12 months hard labour.

AND THEN THERE ARE SOME OTHER VEHICLES...

Wheelbarrow Regulations

If you're planning to transport a wheelbarrow load of dirt from your home to your neighbour's, don't even think about using the sidewalk. That's because St. John's, Newfoundland, banned this form of traffic on city sidewalks many years ago, and the bylaw is still on the books.

Harness Those Hobbies!

Boys will be boys, and often, the bigger the boys, the bigger the toys—or the more dangerous, anyway. According to a bylaw enacted in the town of Morden, Manitoba, in 2003, some toys require regulating or else someone might get hurt. Council in that community decided operating a "gas-powered model vehicle within 300 metres of a residence" is potentially dangerous and therefore outlawed. And people with a passion for flying have to replace their powered airplanes and helicopters with safer and more sedate kites—at least if they want to fly in town. Operating a model aircraft within Morden town limits is now strictly prohibited.

Cool, Clear Waters
And in an effort to keep them that way, the city of Nanaimo, BC, passed a bylaw that is particularly unique to their community. Since March 1995, it has been illegal for anyone to venture into the surrounding waterway in a motorboat whose engine is not equipped with an "exhaust system that permits the exhaust gases from the engine of the motorboat to be expelled directly in to the air without first passing through water." Your motorboat is also required to have a muffler to cool those exhaust fumes and expel them with minimum noise.

Ride 'Em in Safely

Curiously enough, you can still ride your horse into Canmore, as long as you use the public highway and conform to the Traffic Bylaw and Vehicles Act.

Take a Walk on the Right Side
According to a 1922 bylaw, pedestrians in the town of Wilkie, Saskatchewan, had to follow the example of road traffic. They, too, had to pass to the right of any oncoming pedestrians. And anyone willfully breaking this law could face a fine of $25 or 30 days in jail "with or without hard labour."

Not on My Sidewalk

According to a 1922 bylaw, you could not "run, draw or push" a handcart or any other vehicle on sidewalks in the town of Wilkie, Saskatchewan, unless you were repairing it.

Reinforced Bridges

In 1913, it was law in the town of Wilkie, Saskatchewan, for anyone crossing a bridge or culvert with any "traction engine or threshing machine" to reinforce the area with planks 2 inches (5 centimetres) or more in thickness before crossing. Failure to comply with this bylaw could cost you $50 or 30 days in jail.

IT'S NOT EASY BEING GREEN

Environmental Consciousness

It is against the law for motorists in the city of Guelph, Ontario, to allow their vehicle to idle for more than 10 minutes in any 60-minute period. The city bylaw, which was established in 1998, is still in effect.

The city of London, Ontario, is even stricter with their 1999 idling bylaw. Unless you are an on-duty emergency worker or police officer, you have a maximum of five minutes of idling time before you get a ticket.

While the environmental consciousness is admirable, it is unclear how officials manage to monitor vehicle idle time.

Guns and Ammo

"Ride 'em cowboy and away we go!" The words trigger thoughts of guns firing off into a clear blue prairie horizon while riders on horseback gallop off to an unknown destination.

While guns and other weapons are historically all about survival, in an untrained hand they can also be deadly. Thus, the development of firearms laws that to this day cause heated debates across the country.

The following laws are just a few examples of how these regulations developed over the years.

READY, AIM, FIRE!

Keep a Lid on Your Explosives

You couldn't keep more than 50 pounds of gunpowder or other explosives on your property in the town of Ponoka, Alberta, in 1914. The council enacted a bylaw saying that amount of firepower had to be kept a minimum of 100 feet (30.5 metres) from any buildings. You couldn't have more than three barrels of gasoline or kerosene on hand either unless they were located at least 60 feet (18 metres) from any building or stored in iron tanks.

Bombs Away!

In 1964, the town council passed a bylaw making it illegal for anyone to make, distribute or sell a stink bomb in Trenton, Ontario. Break the law and you're fined $25 for the first offence. If you're foolish enough to try it again, the second and subsequent offences will cost you $50. And if you don't pay up your fines after that, you'll be thrown into the clink for up to one month.

Don't Flex That Bow!

Another bylaw enacted in 1956 in Trenton, Ontario, made it illegal to "sell, barter, give, lend, transfer or deliver any bows and arrows to minors within the town of Trenton," unless, of course, the arrow had a rubber-covered tip. And don't plan on setting up for a little target practice either. Minors and adults alike were also forbidden from letting an arrow fly anywhere within the "Corporation of the Town of Trenton." Those caught breaking the bylaw were subject to a $25 fine.

Permit Required

Since 1965, it has been against the law to indiscriminately set explosives to blast rock in the district of Squamish, BC. That's when the council there enacted a bylaw mandating that anyone who wants to blast away at the corner of a mountain must first obtain an explosives permit, complete with a minimum of $150,000 in liability insurance!

Butt Out

In 1914, in the town of Ponoka, Alberta, carrying an open flame into a barn or walking in with a lit cigarette or burning pipe could cost you more than a disastrous fire. Should the town fathers learn of your indiscretion, you could face a $25 fine or up to 30 days in jail, with or without hard labour. While portions of this extensive bylaw were repealed and replaced with updated versions throughout the years, the entire bylaw wasn't repealed until 1998.

You Can't Do That In Public

*Some behaviours are just plain rude, while others
are simply inconsiderate.*

*Strangely enough, what appears to be common sense
to the general public must be made law for the few that
just don't get it.*

DON'T DISTURB THE PEACE

Silence Your Power Saws

Power saws are a noisy tool, and ongoing use is just plain disruptive. In the district of Oak Bay, BC, a 1976 bylaw made it illegal to operate a power saw earlier than 8:00 AM and later than 7:00 PM, Monday to Saturday. But if you found yourself wanting to finish up a few odds and ends requiring the use of a power saw on Sunday, you were out of luck altogether, no matter what the time of day. Sunday was a day of rest, and power saws simply disturbed the peace and quiet of the day. If, on the other hand, you decided to use a good old-fashioned hand saw, that was just fine.

Keep It Down, Would Ya?

An Edmonton, Alberta noise bylaw passed in 1925 made it clear residents couldn't bother their neighbours with any "unusual or unnecessary noise or noise likely to disturb persons in his neighbourhood." Fair enough, you might say. But the same bylaw makes it illegal for any person to "blow or sound or cause to be blown or sounded within the limits of the city of Edmonton, the steam whistle of any locomotive." Since there were exceptions that allowed for train whistles to be blown for safety, based on Alberta statutes of the day, one has to wonder if just anyone was wandering railway yards and blowing steam whistles willy-nilly?

Good Vibrations?

In 2005, council members in Squamish, BC, made a unique addition to their noise bylaw. It is not only illegal to make noise that might "disturb or is liable to disturb the quiet, peace, rest, enjoyment, comfort or convenience of individuals or the public," unnecessary "vibrations" are against the law too. Generally speaking, it's pretty much hush-hush in that community between the hours of 8:00 PM and 8:00 AM.

YOU CAN'T HANG OUT THERE!

No Loitering

Take care of your business and move along. In order to eliminate loitering in the town of Rat Portage (Kenora), Ontario, a bylaw was passed in 1901 making it illegal to park your "horse, cart, carriage, wagon, sleigh or other vehicle" on town streets any longer than absolutely necessary to conduct your business.

In 1976, the county of Halifax, Nova Scotia, passed a similar loitering bylaw, making it illegal for folks to idle about in the halls, washrooms, parking lots or any other common areas of a shopping mall.

Street Sense

Retired gents who enjoyed lounging on benches and watching the world go by had to come up with another pastime. The streets of North Battleford, Saskatchewan, were made for walking— not running, racing or loitering—and town council made these restrictions law in 1906.

IT'S ALL FUN AND GAMES…

Boys Will Be Boys

From the beginning of time, young lads, full of vim and vigour, have always found something to do in what precious spare time they have. If they aren't out capturing frogs or snagging a string of fish, they're likely building forts or planning a treasure hunt. But in 1811, the province of Nova Scotia clamped down on the shenanigans of young boys. That year, it passed an act preventing "boys and others from coasting and sliding down the hills in the streets of Halifax."

More than a century later, in 1916, Yarmouth, Nova Scotia, enacted a bylaw restricting tomfoolery in that community. Throwing snowballs, stones or any other item was against the law. And people swimming in the nearby water hole must either be properly clothed or, if wading without swimwear, not visible to any neighbouring house or street.

KEEP YOUR SHIRT ON

Cover Up!

A municipal bylaw enacted in 1985 in the town of D'Outremont, Québec, made it illegal to appear in public places wearing only your bathing suit. But when one resident heard of the new bylaw, he charged the town with discrimination, saying it "denied him certain fundamental rights that were guaranteed by the Canadian Charter of Rights and Freedoms." The plaintiff, who regularly jogged in nothing more than a bathing suit and routinely sunbathed with his family in public parks, had his claim heard. The end result saw the bylaw declared *ultra vires* (void), based on the Constitution Acts of 1867 and 1982.

Birthday Suit

According to a portion of a 1905 public morals bylaw, it was just fine to bathe in the nude "in any public waters" around the city of Kelowna, BC—just so long as you did so after 9:00 PM and before 6:00 AM. During peak hours, you were required to wear a little more than just your birthday suit or face a fine of up to $100. The entire public morals bylaw was repealed in 1990, but dare to bare your nude body on one of Kelowna's public beaches today and you might still find yourself in hot water with the local officials.

SPLISH SPLASH

No Swimming

In an effort to keep people safe, the city of Kelowna, BC, passed a bylaw in 1944 restricting residents and visitors from bathing and wading in certain parts of Okanagan Lake. The problem is that it isn't always clear which parts of the lake are restricted areas. For example, one portion of the bylaw reads:

"...that part of the said Okanagan Lake between the wire fence on the west side of the Bathing Pool in front of the Grandstand on that Part of District Lot Fourteen (14) in Group One (1) in the City of Kelowna in the Province of British Columbia covered by Certificate of Title No. 35714F leased to The Kelowna Aquatic Association, and a line extending due West into the said Okanagan Lake from a point Six Hundred feet (600') north from the right bank of Mill Creek where the said Mill Creek runs into the said Okanagan Lake..."

To say it's difficult to know where to draw the line (so to speak) is an understatement. And according to one city official, it's not certain if anyone's ever been fined under this bylaw, but people "violate it all the time."

Cleaning Up
Those Acts

It's been said cleanliness is next to godliness.

Canada's founders took this saying to heart, enforcing polite behaviour and outlawing nuisance behaviour like spitting in public.

NO SPITTING!

Keeping City Streets Disease Free

In Yarmouth, Nova Scotia, it was against the law in 1909 for anyone to "expectorate, spit or otherwise deposit saliva" on city streets, sidewalks, stairways, building entrances or any other location where the general public might travel. The goal of the bylaw was to "prevent the spread of disease." Breaking the law could cost $50 in fines or 10 days in jail.

Don't Spit—Anywhere!

In 1917, it was against the law to spit on the sidewalks or in any public place in the town of Trenton, Ontario. And in case you were in any doubt over what that all included, the town fathers were specific. The bylaw clearly states that spitting is not permitted on any "sidewalk or upon the floor of any public building or buildings hall or church."

In 1909, the town council in Yarmouth, Nova Scotia, passed a similar law, making it illegal to spit on the sidewalk or on the floor of any public building "in which 10 or more persons are accustomed to be employed or to congregate or frequent."

Swallow That!
Although a river runs through the sleepy prairie city of Saskatoon, Saskatchewan, no steamship line has ever used the port as its home base. Still, should one set up shop, the city is prepared. In 1910, they passed the Bylaw Prohibiting Spitting in Public Places, and one of the public places cited was the office of any steamship line. Although the law is no longer in the books in its original format, it hasn't been repealed completely. Instead, the Public Spitting, Urination and Defecation Prohibition Bylaw replaced it in 2004.

CLEAN AND DRY

The Common Towel

The year was 1936 and a disease called trachoma had reared its ugly head in the small BC village of Williams Lake. In an effort to snuff out the spread of this and other infections, Williams Lake enacted a bylaw making it illegal for restaurants, schools, hotels and other public areas with a shared bathroom to use a common "roller towel." Anyone not adhering to the bylaw could face a $100 fine—a substantial amount even today, but considerably more so in the dusty, dirty days of the Great Depression.

Business Etiquette

It's a dog-eat-dog world when it comes to succeeding in business, and municipalities across the country pull the strings when it comes to making sure local ventures benefit the community as a whole.

When it comes to best business practices, location—and the governing body regulating commercial etiquette in that location—can spell success or disaster.

THAT'S SHOW BUSINESS!

Licencing Laws

Any actor, singer, circus rider, tightrope walker, acrobat, gymnast, menagerie, hippodrome, dog or pony show or any other such production had to pay for the privilege of stimulating your imagination in the town of Ponoka, Alberta. In 1914, a bylaw made it mandatory for all sorts of entertainers to obtain a performer's licence that, depending on the event, could cost upwards of $50 per day before they even had the privilege of hoisting a tent or holding a show.

Travelling stationary exhibits weren't exempt from the performance licence law either. If you made your livelihood charging people for the chance to see a stuffed two-headed calf, you needed to cough up $10 first.

Everyone Loves a Circus

Entertainers have awed audiences since the beginning of time, and a visiting circus is sure to draw crowds from far and wide. But at least one community made sure any "showmen, circus siders, mountebanks or jugulars [jugglers]" had their paperwork in order before the first tent was pitched in town. The town of Chatham, Ontario, updated their Bylaw Regulating Exhibitions of Waxwork in 1858 to include the above performers, making it unlawful for anyone to strut their stuff before first procuring a licence from the town clerk. If they neglected to do so, it could cost them as much as $20 in fines.

DRIVING
THE RULES HOME

Rules of the Road for Taxicabs

Modest dress is not even a question for taxicab drivers in Halifax, Nova Scotia. According to a 1999 bylaw in that city, wearing socks is a must for cabbies.

But if you think Halifax council is tough, they've got nothing on taxicab regulations passed by the city of Prince George, BC, in 1955. Cabbies there were expressly forbidden from:

☛ allowing any person to "stand on any part of the exterior of the taxicab or sit on the sides or doors" when the cab is "in motion,"

☞ permitting fares jumping into the car when the cab is still "in motion" or

☞ collecting fares while the cab is still moving.

Cabbies also had to have class when it came to attracting passengers. They couldn't hoot and holler at pedestrians. The couldn't "seek employment by repeatedly and persistently driving the taxicab to and fro upon any street...or by hovering in front of any theatre, hall, hotel, public resort, railway or ferry station, or other place of public gathering." Taxi drivers couldn't "loiter or cruise about the street...for the purpose of obtaining passengers," nor could they accept anyone behaving in an "unseemly, disorderly or riotous" manner in their cars.

And speaking of the cab itself, the operator was responsible for disinfecting it weekly—at the very least!

FALSE ADVERTISING

By Any Other Name

Everybody loves a sale. But the name a business gives to its sale is almost as important as what is being sold. In 1960, the city of Halifax, Nova Scotia, enacted a bylaw regulating all "Going Out of Business, Removal of Business, and Fire and Other Altered Goods Sales," and it's still in effect to this day. First and foremost, regardless whether it's being called a "Final Days Sale," a "Lease Expires Sale," a "Liquidation Sale" or any other turn of phrase, if a business advertises it is having a sale because it is going out of business, it must, indeed, be going out of business. A "Removal of Business" sale means that the business is liquidating its stock and will then move to another location. And if a business is having a "Fire and Other Altered Goods Sale," it is only reasonable to expect the items on sale have been damaged in some way. Business owners holding any of these sales are required to obtain a special licence from the city. With the licence, the city provides the business owner with a badge that he or she must then wear in plain sight for the duration of the sale.

You have to be in business for a minimum of six months before the city will sell you the $385 licence for any of these sales. If, on the other hand, you die before your six months is up, the city is lenient on your heirs. They are then allowed to apply for a licence for an out-of-business sale to clear up your estate.

This bylaw has been revisited several times over the years, but even with nine amendments, it's still alive and kicking!

UNDERCOVER SALES

Out of Sight, Out of Mind?

An Edmonton, Alberta bylaw dated August 10, 1931, put a new spin on what might be offensive to the general public. That year council made it illegal for shop owners to display any "pistol, revolver, dirk, dagger, bowie knife, stiletto, metal knuckles, skull cracker, slug shot or other offensive weapon of a like character" in shop windows. The law was repealed in 1996.

Strategic Placement

You can't use sandwich boards to attract folks a few blocks down to your business in Regina, Saskatchewan. A city bylaw states that sidewalk signs must be located "directly in front of the premises being advertised and must not interfere with movement of pedestrians."

Working from Home

Home-based businesses aren't discouraged from setting up shop in the city of Winkler, Manitoba—as long as they do so quietly. The city's home occupations policy states there is to be "no exterior display, no exterior storage of materials, and no exterior indication of the home occupation or variation of the residential character of the principal or accessory building."

SELLING IN THE STREETS

Hawkers and Peddlers

Watch out Watkins. Red alert Amway! Enterprising folk trying to make an extra buck or two in the town of Neepawa better make sure they have a valid business licence before selling door to door or setting up a table at the local farmer's market in Neepawa, Manitoba. Since 1993, a proper licence has been required in that community. There are (as always) some exceptions to the rule. Farmers selling their own fresh produce are exempt from the rule, as are people selling subscriptions for newspapers, magazines or other items approved by the Public Libraries Act and the Municipal Act. If, on the other hand, you're selling fresh Okanagan cherries from a roadside fruit truck, and the farm fresh produce isn't your own, you'll have to make that trip to city hall.

Extra, Extra!

Say goodbye to the days of the street-corner newspaper vendor. In 1950, the town of Carman, Manitoba, made it illegal to sell newspapers, magazines or any other type of publication on town streets or the surrounding highways. Breaking the law could cost you $50. And if you didn't have the money to make good your fine, you could find yourself in jail for a maximum of six months. Needless to say, selling subscriptions didn't pay!

Transient Photographers Must Sign In

While it's perfectly legal for freelance photographers to travel through the city of Cornwall, Ontario, and take photographs for the purpose of someday selling the images to one publication or another, other shutterbugs passing through aren't so lucky.

Transient photographers coming to town for the purpose of shooting school pictures or those promising to capture your baby's most precious moments, for example, need a licence, according to a 2006 bylaw.

Business Etiquette

A public market might typically be a little chaotic, but that doesn't mean there are no rules. The city of Windsor, Ontario, made sure vendors didn't add to the noise level by "calling out their wares," as it were. In 1942, the council of the day passed a bylaw making it illegal for sales folk to stand in the aisles of the public market and advertise their daily specials by calling out to patrons walking by.

FOOD AND DRINK

A Sober Thought

It wasn't until 2002 that the province of British Columbia revamped what some residents in that province felt were some seriously outdated liquor laws. Some of the previous regulations were:

- a patron had to eat if he wanted to order a beer in a restaurant
- a patron had to remain seated while drinking in a restaurant
- a restaurant couldn't call itself a "bar and grill"
- games such as "name that tune" or video trivia games were prohibited in restaurants

Even restaurant decor, such as the height and width of a dance floor, was regulated

After December 2, 2002, these and other regulations were terminated, and restaurants became far more user friendly. Today, if you are dining out and can't finish that nice bottle of wine you ordered, the restaurant is allowed to reseal the bottle for you to take home.

Butchering Bylaws

A 1943 bylaw in the city of Windsor, Ontario, made it illegal for anyone to slaughter an animal or bird of any kind in city streets. And if you were hauling manure or other farm refuse through town, you'd better make sure your load was properly secured. Leaving a trail of leftovers as you passed through could cost you $50.

Original Packing

Butter sold in retail stores in the village of Quesnel, BC, in 1950 had to be sold in its original wrapping. Should a storeowner want to divide the butter into smaller amounts, he had to follow explicit directions approved by the local "Medical Officer of Health."

True Weight

The town constable in Yorkton, Saskatchewan, in 1903 had a rather out-of-the-ordinary annual responsibility. A now obsolete bylaw stated, "It shall be the duty of the Town Constable, at least once in every year, to enter the premises of any baker or vendor of bread, within the said town and weigh the bread found therein." According to the bylaw, each loaf of bread had to weigh a minimum of 2 pounds (907 grams), and the town constable could just drop by unannounced to check if the bread in any local bakery was up to snuff. And while bread was cooling on the rack, its succulent aroma tempting each pedestrian walking by to come in and buy a loaf, patrons who kept their wits about them could ask to have their loaf weighed in front of them—just to be doubly sure they weren't getting cheated out of a slice or two—and the bakery had to have a scale on hand just for that purpose.

The same bylaw also required bakers to follow a strict set of guidelines as far as bread making went. Most importantly, bakers had to make sure their bread was safe. Bakers were forbidden from using any "deleterious material in the making of bread sold or offered or exposed for sale within the said town."

Measuring Up to the Neighbours

In 1996, Edmonton, Alberta, repealed 3884 bylaws that had become obsolete in that city. One of those laws also revolved around the sale of fresh bread. In 1913, Edmonton had two weight restrictions for the bakeries in their community. Loaves were to weigh either 1½ pounds (680 grams) or 3 pounds (1.36 kilograms). Fancy breads could weigh in at 21 ounces (595 grams). The city inspector who made his way through every bakery in that city annually could grant a little leeway, depending on how long the bread was out of the oven. Delivery, on the other hand, was more strictly regulated. The baker planning to deliver his bread must "furnish baskets for the handling of bread, and shall instruct all employees to do the same."

Check That Clock

Butchers in the town of Melville, Saskatchewan, had to check their clocks before slaughtering any animals for human consumption. A bylaw dated 1927 made it illegal to butcher any animal on a weekend. When the dirty deed did occur, it had to take place between the hours of 6:00 PM and 10:00 PM from April 1 to September 30. The rest of the year, butchering had to occur between 1:00 PM and 5:00 PM. The town's meat inspector could issue a special permit from time to time to accommodate exceptional circumstances. Interestingly enough, the bylaw lists no concrete fine for breaking the law.

Got Milk?

Don't plan on selling milk or cream between the hours of 10:00 PM and 7:00 AM in the city of Kingston, Ontario. A 1940 bylaw makes it illegal to do so.

Speaking of Milk...

The last time you could buy farm-fresh milk from a dairy farmer around the city of Grande Prairie, Alberta, was in 1989. That year, city council enacted a bylaw stating it was against the law to sell unpasteurized milk for family consumption.

Something Smells Fishy

Entrepreneurs peddling perch or bartering bass in Trenton, Ontario, had to follow restrictions as early as 1917. That's when the town passed a bylaw restricting anyone from "exposing" or selling fish from their wagon or any other conveyance. The only exception to the bylaw was if a peddler was selling fish at the public market or if he or she was delivering to retail dealers. The fine for breaking the law? $50.

Get Your Fruitcake Here!

Enterprising business folk in the town of Clifton, Alberta, couldn't just go about willy-nilly selling fruitcake, lemon pops, ginger beer or other refreshments. A bylaw deeming it necessary for independent vendors to obtain a business licence was first enacted in 1859, and a licence was even required for a lemonade stand. The town charged the vendor one dollar for the permit, but failure to obtain such a licence could result in prosecution and a $20 fine.

Stock Your Cupboards

Run out of milk on Mondays in the town of Trenton, Ontario, and there was a time when you would have to make do with water until Tuesday morning. In 1960, the town made it law that all grocery stores were to remain closed on Monday.

WHO, WHERE, WHEN?

Location, Location, Location

An entrepreneur wanting to establish an automobile junkyard in Prince Edward Island will have to take several things into consideration when choosing a location. A provincial law states that this type of business can't be located "within a radius of 500 feet (152 metres) of any public park, public playground, public bathing beach, school, church, hospital, cemetery or public hall; within 100 feet (30 metres) of any highway; or within 1000 feet (305 metres) of any residential premises other than those of the applicant for a permit..."

Shop Closing

As recent as the 1990 version of the St. John's, Newfoundland Act, the city council could determine the hours of operation for city retail shops and other businesses as well as what days they must be closed for holidays.

Who Makes the Rules?

The city of Vancouver, BC, initially enacted a bylaw in 1987 called the Shops Closing Bylaw. In a nutshell, any retail outlet can stay open 24 hours a day from Monday to Saturday. The only exception to the rule is if the Licence Bylaw restricts hours of operation. Hmmmm?

Don't Offend the Neighbours

The pioneers who founded this great country of ours survived by making use of everything they came in contact with. An animal was killed for meat, its hide used for warmth, its bones crushed for fertilizer and its tallow boiled for making candles and soap. But when thrifty entrepreneurs began setting up shop and boiling tallow and crushing bones on a large scale, the village of Quesnel, BC, had to step in. What started out as the smell of money turned into an offensive odour for anyone unfortunate enough to live close by. So in 1950, Quesnel council made it law for anyone setting up such a business or any other such "obnoxious or offensive trade" must obtain consent of council first. Likely, this type of stinky enterprise was relegated to the outskirts of town.

Child Labour

In 1916, in the town of Yarmouth, Nova Scotia, a person had to be 16 years old to enter or work in billiard rooms and bowling alleys. The exception to this rule applied to the pin setters in bowling alleys—they could be 12 years old. Of course, only boys were allowed these jobs, and regulations for girls didn't even exist.

Buyer Beware

Palm readers and fortune tellers would have found themselves doing a lot of charity work in 1901 in the town of Rat Portage (Kenora), Ontario, should they have chosen to give residents there a reading. A town bylaw passed that year made it illegal to charge for such services.

No Soliciting

Residents in the city of Beaconsfield, Ontario, are likely thrilled with their council. It is against the law in that city for any "peddler, book agent, canvasser, vendor or public crier [to] at any time do business door to door in any residential zone of the municipality except on behalf of a Beaconsfield nonprofit community organization." And even if you are one of the few exceptions, you still need to pay an annual licencing fee of $30.

DINING OUT

Summer Dining

There's no doubt that restaurant owners have several issues to consider when expanding their business to include sidewalk cafés. Furnishings have to be weatherproof. Pedestrians have to make their way down the street without resorting to walking on the road. Emergency vehicles still have to get by if necessary. For the most part, these considerations are typically a matter of common sense. At the same time, there are always a few unexpected restrictions whenever you deal with your local government.

In the town of Kentville, Nova Scotia, a 2003 bylaw agreed that businesses landscaping around their summer sidewalk café was a good idea, but decided that the landscaping must be of a "temporary nature" unless a business owner had prior written consent from the town. Restaurant owners there were also required to pay a rental charge of 50 cents per ft^2 (0.1 m^2) to run a sidewalk café from May to September.

Fast-food Foreshadowing

Businesses in the city of Windsor, Ontario, are promptly fined if they don't prevent wrappers, containers or even a foul odor from escaping the confines of their operations onto city streets. This bylaw was first passed in 1965.

Open for Business

Restaurant owners in the town of Yarmouth, Nova Scotia, were allowed to open for business on Sundays in 1916, providing they followed a few rules set out by council. They could not sell tobacco, cigars, cigarettes, candy, confectionery, fruit or drinks except tea, coffee, cocoa, chocolate or milk. Breaking the law could cost you $50 or 50 days in jail.

DIRTY BUSINESS

Butt Out

The town fathers in Melville, Saskatchewan, seemed to have a somewhat advanced sense of awareness where the health of their youngsters was concerned. In 1955, a bylaw was passed to "limit and regulate the number of tobacco advertising signs in the ice stadium." Only one company was allowed to advertise its brand of tobacco at any one time, and for the privilege, they were responsible for supplying and maintaining the stadium time clock.

Coal, Hard Facts

Heating your home with coal was no easy feat in 1936. That year, the town of Carman, Manitoba, enacted a bylaw requiring coal-sellers to sell their product by weight. To avoid any discrepancy, all loads of coal were to be weighed on the town scales before delivery, and the town weigh-master would collect the princely sum of 10 cents per load to add to the town's coffers. The coal seller would receive a ticket certifying the load's true weight from the weigh-master, and that ticket would in turn be given to the end user on delivery. Try to break free of the red tape, and the town could slap you with a $50 fine.

In 1943, another bylaw added restrictions to the amount draymen could charge for delivering coal or wood within Carman's town limits. If they were delivering wood they couldn't charge more than 50 cents per cord. Coal would be delivered for not less than 50 cents and not more than 80 cents per ton or portion thereof. Talk about complicated!

Made to Shop

Shopping carts in the town of Kenora, Ontario, became such an unsightly nuisance in 1992 that town council had no choice but to take clear and decisive action. A bylaw passed that prohibited anyone from abandoning shopping carts on private property without the consent of the property owners. It was also against the law to abandon shopping carts on town property. Unfortunately, the owner of the shopping cart, and not the patron who abandoned it, would face a $15 fine should they want the cart returned.

Mind Your
Manners

Proper etiquette was an important consideration to the courageous men and women who pioneered this vast and wild country. To be well mannered was a sign of civilization—like the difference between using a fork and using your fingers to eat your dinner.

Today, it's a generally accepted fact that you're likely to hear "foul language" while walking city streets, so there's no need for a bylaw on the matter—a sad commentary on society, really. At the same time, people don't commonly spit inside public buildings anymore. Again, there's no longer any need for a law on the matter—thankfully! At the very least, it's interesting to see how times have changed.

WATCH YOUR MOUTH

Foul!

A foul mouth could cost you $50 or get you locked away for 30 days in the town of Falher, Alberta, in 1957. That year, the town council passed a bylaw "to promote peace and good behaviour" in their community.

Be Nice to the Lady

In 1898, you'd better have known what you're talking about when you suggested a lady in the North-West Territories was unfaithful to her husband, unchaste or guilty of reckless extravagance of any kind. If you were lying, you could face legal action, whether the young lady slandered could prove any personal damages or not.

The Name Says It All

Council members of the village of Nakusp, BC, have the sole right to determine the name of any new municipal parks. The 1988 bylaw highlights the fact that the village elite want to honour "persons or events in a tangible and lasting manner" and will use the naming of parks for that purpose.

MAINTAINING MORALITY

Public Morals

In 1893, maintaining public morals was a major concern for the town of Sudbury, Ontario, and to snuff out any potential problems, the council of the day enacted a bylaw addressing some of their concerns. Morality laws, as these laws came to be called, were common in communities across the country.

- ☞ Unless you were announcing the beginning of a religious service of some sort, the ringing of bells was strictly prohibited.
- ☞ Despite the lack of organized animal rights groups in the late 19th century, the town of Sudbury was serious about making sure animals under their jurisdiction didn't come to unnecessary harm. Residents were expressly forbidden from hosting, running, baiting or inciting in any way fights between any "bull, bear, dog, cock or other animal (whether of domestic or wild nature or kind)."

☛ Unless you were one of "her Majesty's soldiers," an on-duty militia member, a sheriff, a police officer or a member of a rifle club in the midst of target practice, you'd better not even think about firing "any cannon, gun, pistol or other fire alarm."

☛ You didn't want to let the town fathers catch you bathing or washing that naked body of yours in anything deemed "public water." You could be in deep trouble if you did—not to mention being embarrassed at being caught with your britches down.

☛ If you didn't like something town council was addressing, letting your representatives know was a little tricky. Disrupting the "order or solemnity of the meeting" was against the law.

☛ If you happened to own a wolf, bear or other wild animal, or were perhaps animal-sitting for a friend, you'd better not let your charge out of your sight. Should the animal happen to wander the streets of Sudbury, you could face a $50 fine.

☛ Down on your luck? You'd better make sure a member of the clergy or two justices of the peace signed a certificate stating that you were "a deserving object of charity" before you started strolling highways and public lanes or knocking on doors for a bit of bread or a piece of cheese. Without this document, begging for alms was prohibited.

☛ Wondering about your future? In 1893, you had to keep on wondering until it happened. Fortunetellers of any kind likely didn't stop by the town of Sudbury often, since they were prohibited from charging for their services.

Prim and Proper

In the interest of "peace, order and good government," the city of Moose Jaw, Saskatchewan, enacted a modern version of the old morality laws in 1999. People in that city can't

- deface a memorial plaque or sign,
- build a fence using barbed wire,
- leave a trail of nails, tacks or glass behind them while walking down city sidewalks,
- damage the bark of or uproot any trees and
- allow their doors swing out "over any part of any sidewalk or street within the city."

Behave yourself

Proper behaviour is something that's expected of a good citizen, but in the town of Jasper, Alberta, it's an expectation that's legislated. Inciting someone to fight, using profanity, defacing property or being generally annoying is enough to earn a fine—shouting obscenities alone will cost you a minimum of $150. Curiously enough, this isn't an old bylaw. It was just passed in August 2005.

ASK NICELY

Please, Sir?

Beggars in the town of Rat Portage (Kenora), Ontario, would go hungry if they didn't follow the rules. In 1901, it was made law that beggars going door to door or asking for food or money in the town streets had to have a certificate signed by "a priest, clergyman or minister of the gospel or two justices of the peace" allowing them to do so. It was also the responsibility of the beggar to have his certificate reviewed and renewed every six months if he wanted to continue to receive alms.

By the Book

Panhandling in Saskatoon, Saskatchewan, is perfectly legal. But panhandlers have to follow a few rules first. They can't coerce or pester people walking by, they can't bother someone sitting in a parked vehicle or one that's stopped at a red light and they can't beg for money on a Saskatoon transit bus. They also can't obstruct the doorway to a "bank, credit union, or trust company" or an automated teller machine, bus stop or bus shelter. If they do, they're going to find themselves in considerable trouble, since the fine for a first offense is $100. This bylaw was first enacted in 1999 but has been updated as recently as 2003.

ALL WET

No Swimming

Nude swimming was just fine at the turn of the 20th century in Summerside, PEI, as long as you took a dip between the hours of 8:30 PM and 7:00 AM. Any other time of the day, you'd better have been properly attired for the occasion.

A 1912 bylaw in the town of Edson, Alberta, similarly restricted bathing and swimming in town limits to between the hours of 9:00 PM and 6:00 AM. The interesting twist to this bylaw is it didn't only restrict swimming for those doing so in the nude.

DECENCY LAWS

Going Topless

In 1996, a young woman in Guelph, Ontario, decided to walk down city streets topless. It was, after all, really hot that day. While some folk didn't find her attire suitable, the Ontario Court of Appeal decided, on a unanimous vote, that the lady in question hadn't violated any "community standards" by going topless. Whether this was a good choice or not depends on who you talk to, but it's definitely still a matter of debate.

The Oldest Profession

Most communities with morality laws made some reference to the fact that it was against the law for folks to visit a house of ill repute or avail themselves of the services of a prostitute. A 1912 bylaw in Edson, Alberta, however, addressed citizens' concerns over "common prostitutes or night walkers." If a suspected prostitute was discovered wandering "in the fields, public streets or highways, lanes or places of public meeting or gathering of people," she was expected to "give satisfactory account of herself." I'm sure all will agree with Ann Dechambeau of the town of Edson when she said, "I'm not sure what a satisfactory account is!"

Keep It Covered!

Morality laws in the town of Rat Portage (Kenora), Ontario, were quite explicit when it came to public indecency. A bylaw passed in 1901 made exhibitionism illegal. You also couldn't make or display any "obscene picture, plate, print, drawing, statue or any other indecent exhibition" within the town, nor could you wash your naked body in any "public water."

AND MORE GOOD MANNERS...

Privy Business

It simply wasn't considered proper to move an outhouse in the town of Summerside, PEI, between the hours of 4:00 AM and 10:00 PM in 1897. After all, doing so would cause quite a stink!

Noise Pollution

Blowing horns, playing football, and using insulting language were all lumped together in the town of North Battleford, Saskatchewan, in 1906. All these activities, as well as ringing bells, playing cricket, baseball, lacrosse or any other game, swearing or using any kind of "loud, blasphemous" or abusive language, were against the law.

Bury Your Dead

Your neighbours are likely sad at the death of your loved one, but that doesn't mean you can exhibit the body in public and hope that sympathy turns into dollars and cents. A 1901 morality bylaw in the town of Rat Portage (Kenora), Ontario made it illegal for "deformed, malformed or deceased" persons to be displayed publicly for the purpose of gathering money from public sympathy.

Shhhhh...Don't Get Too Excited

Another 1901 morality bylaw in the town of Rat Portage placed a few restrictions on celebrations, including weddings. The party couldn't get too carried away, as any loud jubilation was considered a disturbance of the peace.

Private Parking

A bylaw passed by the town of Jasper, Alberta, in 2002 makes it illegal for tourists to camp out in the grocery store parking lot or on any other public land within town limits, no matter how many "no vacancy" signs they might have passed before nightfall. Close your eyes, even for just a few hours, and you could wake up to a fine.

Keeping Critters Happy

If you think rules for people are complex, the ins and outs of maintaining livestock, not to mention keeping a family pet, can prove to be just as complicated.

For some of the past and present bylaws listed below, you can easily imagine the rationale behind them, but others seem a tad extreme. Just take a look and you'll see what I mean.

HORSING AROUND

Oliphant's Amazing Law of Horses

In 1908, a barrister-at-law named George Henry Hewitt Oliphant authored a book, *The Law of Horses*, using British common law and applying it here in Canada. The following are just a few of the interesting dos and don'ts of that era:

- ☞ It was okay to hunt fox, otter or other "noxious animals," even if it took you through your neighbour's property. That's because these animals were considered "noisome vermin" and "injurious to the commonwealth."

- ☞ A horse injuring a person was a serious legal matter, even if that horse belonged to the local fire department. According to an 1872 case, a nosey voyeur was checking out a neighbourhood fire and was subsequently injured by an unattended horse. The judge found the Montréal fire department that owned the animal was liable for damages.

- ☞ Meandering bees killed two horses in one 1906 case. The court found the beekeeper liable for damages. After all, he should have known that his bees would wander and could pose a threat to his neighbours or passing traffic.

- ☞ Innkeepers in the 19th century were responsible for providing a safe place for horses belonging to their patrons. In one 1858 case, an innkeeper was held responsible for the actions of his staff, who were believed to have shorn a horse's mane and tail while the animal was in his care.

- ☞ Citing a law of King Athelstan, "merchandizing on the Lord's Day" was expressly forbidden. No "tradesman, artificer, workman, labourer or other person whatsoever, shall do or exercise any worldly labour, business or work of their ordinary callings upon the Lord's Day." However, anyone who wasn't a horse dealer could enter into a contract to sell a horse on a Sunday.

Road Travel Only

In 1967, the village of Airdrie, Alberta, first passed a bylaw restricting horses and riders from travelling on "sidewalks, boulevards and lawns." They were limited to street and alley travel only.

Secure Your Horse

If you plan to leave your horse unattended for any length of time, you'd better not plan on tying her to the nearest lamppost, water pump or hydrant. A 1901 bylaw in the town of Rat Portage (Kenora), Ontario, made it illegal to do so. Horses pulling a wagon, carriage or any other vehicle were also required to have two or more bells securely attached around their necks.

Registered Horses

Horse owners in city limits and within 1.6 kilometres of St. John's, Newfoundland, must pay a licence fee by July 2nd of every year. If you purchase a horse after July 1, you have to licence the horse before using it.

Chow-time Etiquette

Want to feed your horse after a long drive into town? In Yarmouth, Nova Scotia, a law was passed in 1918 making it illegal to feed your horse on the street "except by a nose bag."

It was also against the law to wash your vehicle while it was parked on the street.

Residents with horse-drawn vehicles such as carriages, wagons, sleighs and others, whether the conveyances are used only for personal use on private property or used for hire, must register these vehicles by July 2 of each year. These bylaws were still found in the 1990 version of the City of St. John's Act.

LIVELY LIVESTOCK

Control Your Critters

The municipal council of the town of Lloydminster, Alberta, read farmers the riot act in 1908. That was the year they made it law for animal owners "or any person having the custody or care of any horse, mule, jack, cattle, sheep, goat, swine, rabbit, goose, turkey, duck or poultry" to keep their critters off town streets at all times. Town fathers took great care to list every possible livestock of the day, and there were no exceptions to the rule. Those who broke the law faced a $20 fine or seven days in jail. Curiously, dogs and cats were absent from the list. And one can't help but wonder what might happen to any wild bunny bouncing through town.

By 1935, it was no longer legal for animals of any kind, "horse, mule, ass, cattle, sheep, pig, goat or goose," to run at large within the village limits of Falher, Alberta. Animals not on their owner's property were to be under "immediate, continuous and effective control" of a caregiver and "securely tethered."

In 1985, the city of Guelph, Ontario, passed a bylaw stipulating rules for keeping ducks, geese, poultry or pigeons in city limits. The approved pens couldn't be located closer than 50 feet (15 metres) from "any school, church or dwelling house not including the owner's dwelling house."

Keep Your Critters Penned

Allow your cattle to roam the streets of Port Coquitlam, BC, and you could be in for a pile of trouble. First, there's a fine of up to $2000, six months in jail or both. Then there are the initial pound keeper fees of $35, followed by an additional $20 a day for food and care. If the cow in question is a milking Holstein, the pound keeper must milk the animal twice daily, but you won't see a drop of it, since whatever is collected goes directly to the pound keeper to reward him for his efforts.

The same fees apply to other large animals, including stallions, horses, donkeys, bulls, goats, sheep, swine and mules. Geese, ducks, fowl, poultry and rabbits cost their owners a little less, with an impound fee of $10 and a daily care rate of $2.50. Curiously enough, this bylaw was first enacted in November 1970 and is still on the books.

Cow Census

In 1935, the city of Kelowna, BC, passed a bylaw requiring farmers to register all cows kept within city limits with the city clerk every 12 months. The registration included an inspection from the Medical Health Officer of not only the cow, but also the owner and all members of the family. This bylaw wasn't repealed until 1990.

Dairy Dos and Don'ts

The town of Cochrane, Ontario, was pretty specific when it came to regulations surrounding the production and sale of milk. In 1924, if a dog or cat happened to wander into the barn area or milk house, the farmer was effectively breaking the law. And it could cost as much as $50.

Animal Farm

Pound keepers in the city of Weyburn, Saskatchewan, had an entirely different set of responsibilities back in 1924 than they do today. According to a bylaw enacted that year, the pound keeper's job was to impound animals running loose. However, the term "animal" referred to everything except dogs and cats. Any animal—bull, stallion, horse, mule or the like—found wandering about with no owner in site could be captured by anyone noticing the vagrant and be brought to the city pound. Should the wandering animal trample through a farmer's field of ripened wheat or cause some other damage, the injured party had to submit a written complaint to the pound keeper in duplicate, together with a dollar amount for the cost of damages. The impounded animal was destined to remain behind bars until its owner paid his debt in full or until the court ordered the animal sold. The proceeds from the sale of such an animal was divided between the costs of the sale itself and any monies due to the original complainant.

To the individual initially delivering the wandering animal to the pound, a set fee would be paid as follows:

- ☛ Stallion or bull: $5.00
- ☛ Boar or ram: $2.00
- ☛ Horse, mule, jack, ox, or cow: $0.50
- ☛ Swine (other than a boar), calf or sheep: $0.25
- ☛ Domestic fowl: $0.10

The pound keeper added a receiving charge of anywhere from 10 to 50 cents for each animal, along with a daily maintenance charge of a similar amount. Add to that the notification fee of 50 cents, the delivery of a notice of sale for 50 cents and posting notices of the sale throughout town at $1.00, and pretty soon the owner was out of pocket a considerable portion of the animal's worth.

Whatever was left over from the proceeds of the sale would be returned to the original owner—once that ownership was proven.

A Pound of Many Species

According to a 1970 bylaw, the city of St. John's, Newfoundland council may, when required, establish facilities for the "impounding of horses, horned cattle, sheep and swine or other domestic animals which may be found straying, or at large, in streets or parks of the city."

Animal Access

Sidewalks in the city of Sault Ste. Marie are for pedestrians, period. Don't even think about taking your dog team and sled for a boot along the sidewalk. Sleds, toboggans and all other vehicles are banned from the walkways. The only exception to the rule is if you need to pass over a paved or plank sidewalk to enter a property.

Animals aren't welcome on the street either. So if you need to drive a herd of cattle, sheep or pigs, you can't use any of Sault Ste. Marie's city streets.

Special Permission

Since sheep roam about freely in some parts of the city of Fort Saskatchewan, Alberta, a herding dog is needed to keep them all in line. And to herd sheep, a dog needs to be able to roam about freely, and it isn't always under the direct control of a handler. So in 2002, the council reviewed its animal control bylaw to allow for the free movement of herding dogs.

Animal Control

Farmer Joe may have thought that by securing a cow bell around Ol' Bessie's neck, he'd have a clearer idea of her whereabouts, but town fathers in Orillia, Ontario, had a different idea. In 1883, they passed a bylaw making it illegal for cows to run "at large with bells attached to them" within town limits. Farmers had to be even more attentive to their livestock after another bylaw passed later that same year restricted the time of day cows could wander through town unattended.

In 1897, farmers faced another roadblock after a new bylaw prevented them from the "leading of, driving or pasturing of horses, cows or other horned cattle upon the sidewalks or boulevards in the town of Orillia."

Two years later, Orillia farmers had yet another area of their farming practices to pay a little more attention to—they had to be careful how they bred their horses. A bylaw passed that year made it illegal for farmers to breed their mares and studs "on or in any of the streets, hotels, yards or parks of the town." Basically, no more equine nookie in public view.

FINES FOR SWINE

The Problem with Pigs

In 1914, town council declared that swine pens in Ponoka, Alberta, should be built a minimum of 300 feet (91.5 metres) from any home or business, and "no more than two pigs of any one age shall be kept in any one pen." If your neighbours complained about any offensive odours wafting in from your direction, you could end up with town officials at your doorstep. Swine pens were to be kept "dry and free from offensive odours" at all times.

It wasn't until 1952 that the village of Airdrie, Alberta, took action when it came to dealing with livestock kept within their village limits. A bylaw enacted that year made it illegal to have any kind of livestock in the village. The only exceptions to the rule were dogs, cats, parrots and canaries "providing the council [did] not consider them objectionable." In unique circumstances, council could give special permission for an individual to contravene the law, but they'd have to reapply for this special permission every year, and council members could change their minds at any time, despite their initial approval. By 1968, "no horses, cattle or chickens" were allowed—under any circumstance—to be kept in any residential area of Airdrie.

THESE LAWS ARE FOR THE BIRDS

No Fowl Odours

Bird lovers in the city of Kingston, Ontario, have a list of rules to adhere to if they want to keep pigeons on their property. A 1957 bylaw stated that people with bird shelters must thoroughly wash the inside walls, ceilings, and floors at least once a year, clean droppings daily, turn the earth in the outside areas of the bird house regularly and dispose of collected bird droppings at least twice a week.

People with pigs weren't so lucky. In 1963, it was illegal to keep any kind of pig—even pets of the potbellied persuasion—if you lived within Kingston city limits.

While limitations were put on pig possession in the village of Lloydminster, Alberta, as early as 1918, the council didn't ban the beasts altogether. Instead, householders in that village were only allowed two pigs on their premises at any one time. The animals had to be kept in an appropriate pen located "not less than 100 feet from any dwelling." Just two years later, that bylaw was repealed, and pigs were no longer allowed in town under any circumstances.

The town of Cochrane, Ontario, passed an outright "no pigs allowed" bylaw in 1922. There was one difference, though. Swine could pass through the town, as long as they didn't stay more than five days.

Feathered Friends?

Birdhouses, birdbaths or bird feeding stations are okay in the city of Moose Jaw, Saskatchewan. But just try to raise any livestock, and you're barking up an entirely different tree.

According to a 1998 bylaw, you can't even have more than two hamsters or guinea pigs in your home without breaking the law.

Foul-feathered Frustrations

No, it's not the Wild West. But you might still hear a shotgun blast from time to time in the town of Carman, Manitoba. Because of an overabundance of nuisance birds, town council passed a law allowing animal control officers to shoot to kill… crows and grackles, that is. The law came into effect in 2001.

Fowl!

It was against the law for homeowners in the village of Quesnel, BC, to keep poultry or any other fowl in their home—and that included the basement! Business owners and shopkeepers had to follow the same rules, according to a 1950 bylaw.

Clip Those Feathers

If you lived in the town of Cochrane, Ontario, in 1913 and planned on keeping poultry, you couldn't let them wander—or fly—off your property. If your feathered friends got onto public property, you could face a $5.00 fine.

Don't Feed the Birds

Stroll along the shores of Lake Banook or Little Abro Lake in the city of Dartmouth, Nova Scotia, and chances are you'll meet a few feathered friends. But if you're inclined to share your sunflower seeds or toss a slice or two of bread in their direction, think again. It is illegal to feed the birds if you're within 50 feet (15 metres) of the lakeshore.

Not Good for the Goose

At an April 1853 town council meeting in Yarmouth, Nova Scotia, it was made law that geese were no longer allowed to waddle about freely in town limits. The penalty for ignoring the law? Five shillings.

Pigeon Police

Though a little more difficult to regulate, feathered fowl aren't exempt from a few rules of their own. A bylaw is still on the books making it illegal to feed the pigeons in Sault Ste. Marie, even on your own personal property. It's considered a public nuisance in that city for pigeons to land on private property, defecate when flying overhead or be too noisy.

DOMESTIC AND NOT-SO-DOMESTIC PETS

Dangerous Animals

If you want to own a pit bull in Grande Prairie, Alberta, you'd better check out the town's animal bylaws. Owning anything labelled a "Restricted and Dangerous Animal" means you'd better have a minimum of $500,000 in liability coverage just in case that pooch of yours bites the neighbour—or anyone else for that matter.

Not Allowed

In case there was any doubt, a 1988 bylaw in the city of Guelph, Ontario, outlined specifically the kinds of animals the ordinary Joe could keep as a pet. Kangaroos and opossums, gorillas and monkeys, wild cats and dogs, mongooses, civets and gents, skunks, weasels, otters and badgers, bears, raccoons, hyenas, seals and walruses, snakes of the pythonidae and boidae family, ostriches, rheas and cassowaries, eagles, hawks and owls, anteaters, sloths and armadillos, alligators and crocodiles, and all bats were among the banned species. Interestingly enough, while it is not a law, the town of Gladstone, Manitoba, encourages its residents to make bat houses to attract the flying mammals since bats eat mosquitoes, and mosquitoes carry the West Nile virus.

Here's One for the Birds

Cat owners in the town of Fort Saskatchewan, Alberta, had some rather unique rules to follow in 1938. Out of great concern for the preservation of the area's song birds, the town council of the day enacted a bylaw making it mandatory for every cat to wear a collar equipped with a bell at all times. Since cats were considered "an enemy to the songbirds," a wandering feline flittering through town without the legislated bell around his neck could find himself dodging bullets. The bylaw stated the feline offender could be "shot at large." Amazingly, Fort Saskatchewan had this bylaw on the books for 20 years before it was repealed.

Out of the same concern, the town of Stavely, Alberta, enacted a cat-belling bylaw the same year. In fact, they announced themselves the first community in the world to have such a law, responding to concerns at the time from the Audubon Society about deaths of songbirds because of domestic cats. Stavely's bylaw also allowed for the shooting of cats. Council even paid a man named Halvar "Red" Rostrum to shoot every cat or kitten he found wandering about without a bell—as long as they were shot before noon.

King of the North?

If you live in Yellowknife, Northwest Territories, and you are pondering the prospect of welcoming a furry friend of the lion persuasion into your family, think again. After a resident's pet lion attacked two people in that community in 1977, the city council enacted a bylaw making it illegal to keep a lion within city limits, and any such feline discovered could be destroyed. The owner of the pet lion responsible for initiating the bylaw was given 30 days to find a new home for his feline protégé. While one is hard-pressed to imagine another family setting up house with a lion in tow, the bylaw remains in effect to this day—just in case.

Speaking of Cats

In Taber, Alberta, all cats six months and older must be licenced—and if they aren't "altered," then the cost to the owner is considerably more than the $15 for a cat that's been spayed or neutered. All cats must wear a "harness and leash with a licence attached" whenever they are outside their homes, and any cats found wandering that aren't "altered" will be part of the town's trap-neuter-release program, where wandering unlicenced cats "will be spayed or neutered if appropriate." A cat might make be returned to its owner—if he or she coughs up the money to cover the costs. Otherwise, the cat will be adopted out.

Population Control, Animal Style

You might be a pet-loving family, but if you live in Inuvik, Northwest Territories, you'd better pick and choose your companions carefully. Unless you have a kennel or a registered dog team, you are forbidden from having "more than three animals exceeding the age of five months" in any one household or property, and that includes hamsters, parrots and guinea pigs. The bylaw, enacted in 1998, still requires residents with dog teams to register each and every animal by listing their name, type, colour, age and sex on a formal application form.

Rats!

You can own a pet rat in Port Coquitlam, BC, but there are limits. More than four pet rats or another combination of pet rodents in one household, and you're breaking the law. The penalty? A $2000 fine, six months in jail or both.

Keep It To Yourself!

Your pet might be lovable, but if it's a snake, tarantula or scorpion, chances are your neighbour or anyone else passing by won't be in too much of a hurry to see it. And in 1990, the city of Kingston, Ontario, made it illegal to carry this type of pet in any public place, considering it a public nuisance. The only exceptions to the rule were schools, zoos or veterinary offices. Anyone transporting a snake, tarantula or scorpion was required to place the creature in a cloth bag to be then "contained inside a durable box having a lid, which is securely fastened." Breaking the law could make a $2000 dent in your bank account.

Species Specifications

It is currently against the law to keep a pet poisonous snake in the city of Dartmouth, Nova Scotia. Nonpoisonous snakes are fine, unless they grow to an adult length of more than 2 feet

(61 centimetres). Pet scorpions, tarantulas and black widow spiders are also illegal. And it's against the law for any pet store in Dartmouth to sell these creatures.

The town of Bedford, Nova Scotia, takes these regulations a step further. Circuses or any other travelling shows passing through aren't even allowed to bring their pythons, scorpions or spiders while travelling through town.

The city of Guelph, Ontario, enacted a bylaw in 1978 making it illegal for anyone to have a pet snake that isn't indigenous to Canada. Zoos and research facilities are exempt.

The city of Halifax, Nova Scotia, has a similar bylaw that was enacted in 1992. While it appears residents can have pets outlawed in some of their neighbouring communities, they'd better keep their reptiles under lock and key. Should a pet snake end up wandering city streets, its owner could face a fine of up to $500—if anyone could find the snake's home, that is!

Pooper Scoopers

While it's in good taste to clean up after your pooch when he relieves himself on someone else's property while you're out for a walk, many dog owners choose to turn the other cheek, so to speak. Because of such inconsiderate behaviour, the county of Halifax, Nova Scotia, passed a bylaw in 1989 making it a fineable offence to ignore your duties. Now, if your neighbour catches you looking the other way, you could find yourself faced with a $100 fine or a 30-day jail sentence.

WILD KINGDOM

Gator Wrestling

It is a Criminal Code violation to fight or bait animals or birds, or encourage, aid or assist an individual fighting or baiting animals or birds. Strangely enough, a video depicting an alligator show at Winnipeg's Red River Exhibition might have disturbed one viewer, but despite visible contact between the "showman" and his alligator, the judge in the 1997 case did not find that there was sufficient contact to suggest any fighting or wrestling had occurred.

Bee Serious?

Urban dwellers may have few farming options open to them, but several communities in Canada allow beekeepers to run an apiary within city limits. In some places, a windowsill apiary can be operated, even in a high-rise apartment! Of course, there are laws for this type of operation. Vernon, BC, has a bylaw for the "keeping of bees." Beekeepers must ensure their hives don't pose a risk to their neighbours or anyone passing by on public property, and they must keep any damage to neighbouring private or public property "to a minimum." Vancouver, BC, has a similar bylaw for windowsill beehives.

Don't Touch a Hare

Circus performers and exhibitors had to check the bylaws in Digby, Nova Scotia, before they coaxed a lion to leap through a circle of fire or encouraged a bear troupe dressed in pink tutus to dance for the camera. In 1996, council enacted the Circus Performance Bylaw, making it illegal to encourage animals to perform "tricks, fight or participate in exhibitions or performances for the amusement or entertainment of an audience." There are exceptions. Magicians can still pull rabbits out of their hats, viewers can still bet on horse races and long live the rodeo!

Rules of
Employment

*Life is nothing if not complicated. And while running
a business obviously has its array of ups and downs, who
knew just hiring staff could lead to such a list of
interesting bylaws?*

EARNING AN HONEST DOLLAR

Child Labour

Young lads hoping to support their families in 1906 couldn't get a job in a coalmine in the province of Alberta, unless they were at least 12 years old and able to read, write and were "familiar with the rules of arithmetic." According to the same provincial bylaw, no girl of any age could be employed in a coalmine.

Child Labour Laws

Edmonton, Alberta, was pretty strict when it came to establishing child labour laws within the confines of that city in 1909. Young boys had to be at least 10 years old and young girls had to be 16 before they could sell newspapers, magazines or "small wares." They also couldn't operate as a "boot-black," or shoe shiner, without meeting the age qualifications.

Youngsters meeting the minimum age requirements still needed a valid licence from the city and had to wear an official badge at all times when they were working. To obtain these prerequisites, the child wanting employment had to obtain a written statement from their school principal outlining the status of their attendance, and the principal had to further explain that the youth in question was "of the normal development of a child of his age and physically fit for such employment, and that such principal or chief executive officer approves the granting of permit and badge to such child."

Further, no youth could work after 9:00 PM or before 6:00 AM. And any child working without the appropriate licence and badge or working outside of the specified time limits would be arrested and would face a trial in juvenile court.

Licences expired on January 1 of each year, and youth would have to reapply in order to keep working. The badges worn by these youngsters also listed their next-of-kin information along with their personal description.

Women's Work

In 1926, it would cost you more than just an hourly wage to employ a woman in the town of Wilkie, Saskatchewan. Following The Female Employment Act of the Revised Statues of Saskatchewan of that year, Wilkie council made it law that every business wanting to employ "female labour" had to apply for a licence from the town clerk and pay a $1.00 fee. The licence expired on December 31 of each year, so if you had a great employee and wanted to keep her for another year, you'd have to cough up another dollar.

Odds and Ends

A jaded individual might believe you can't breathe without breaking the law. Who'd have thought someone would come up with a law about fighting alligators, for example?

Or what about the guy who just can't keep himself from tempting fate by doing something most of us would find irrational?

If you can imagine something, chances are someone has tried it somewhere. And with each fate-testing adventurer, another law is likely born.

ELECTION TIME

No Excuses

The residents of Fort Saskatchewan, Alberta, have historically been encouraged to get out and vote on election day—so much so that the town council in 1969 passed a bylaw eliminating one more reason someone might be waylaid en route to the voting station. That bylaw prohibited the "sales of liquor within the municipality on voting or election day." Sheryl Exley, administrative assistant to the mayor and council in that city, noted that it appears this bylaw was only in effect for one year.

Advance Polls

Railway men were perhaps the first to get the chance to vote at an advance poll in the early days of the 20th century—after all, they were often away more than they were home. In 1919, the town of Cochrane, Alberta, passed a bylaw opening advance polls for three days prior to election day. The law was repealed several years later.

CANADIAN, BY THE RULES

The Value of Women

Believe it or not, it wasn't until 1929 that women were considered "persons" under Canadian law. While Canadian women made considerable accomplishments prior to that date, legally they were thought of as little more than property.

A Quiet Patriotism
Letting the Canadian flag flying in your front yard snap in the wind is against the law according to one judge in Collingwood, Ontario. Apparently, a 1999 incident resulted in a schoolteacher being summoned to court because of his wayward, noisy Canadian flag.

A LITTLE RESPECT

In His Honour

With few exceptions, retail shops, businesses and industries throughout the city of Edmonton, Alberta, were to keep their doors locked and businesses closed on Friday, February 15, 1952, according to a city bylaw passed just four days earlier. Sadly, it wasn't because of a festive occasion. Instead, the day was set aside as a day of mourning for King George VI.

Although it was obviously a one-time occurrence, the bylaw wasn't repealed until 1996.

Honouring Our Heroes

The War Memorial Monument in the city of Charlottetown, PEI, is a testament to the gift of freedom our veterans and war dead gave us through their service. It's meant for citizens to come and pay their respects and ponder the many sacrifices these brave people made. It is not meant to be used as a crash pad. According to a 2003 bylaw, anyone taking up "permanent or temporary abode" at the monument could be fined between $100 and $5000, spend up to 90 days in jail or both.

In Remembrance

Folks in Medicine Hat, Alberta, remember their veterans on November 11 in a unique way. All retail and wholesale businesses, with the exception of pharmacies and other essential services, are required to remain closed from 9:00 AM to noon under a 1985 bylaw.

NEAT AND TIDY

That's Not Junk

The 1957 Chevy frame you have sitting in your front yard might be your future dream car, but if it doesn't have a current licence plate, is spotted with rust and is in plain sight of other residents, then it's considered a junked vehicle in Regina, Saskatchewan. A bylaw in that city states owners of junked vehicles must "remove them, place them in a garage or licence them."

Hold Down Your Hay!

Loose hay, straw or other feed blowing about in the village of Lloydminster, Alberta, was considered a fire hazard and a nuisance, so the council took decisive action to prevent that from happening. In 1919, a bylaw was enacted that required farmers to keep hay and other feed enclosed in a building. Failure to do so could cost you $20 or 30 days in the nearest "common gaol."

Serious Business

Composting may be a great environmentally friendly option, but folks in the town of Legal, Alberta, better know how to do it correctly. A portion of their nuisance bylaw states it's an offence for property owners to place "cat feces, dog feces, animal parts or animal meat on a composting pile."

The same bylaw makes it an offence for residents to have an outside light that shines "directly into the living or sleeping area of an adjacent dwelling house."

Garage Sale No-nos

Whether you were planning on holding a garage sale in the town of Ponoka, Alberta, or just wanting to donate a few things to the local thrift store, it was once law that you had to have any items of clothing laundered first. A bylaw dating back to 1939 made it illegal to sell second-hand clothes, boots or accessories without cleaning them first. And if you thought tossing your used clothing in the washing machine should do it, you couldn't have been more wrong. All items had to be "disinfected by a method approved of by the local Board of Health." Dare to defy the bylaw, and you could be fined $50—likely more than what you could have made at the garage sale. Exactly how a bylaw officer would know if the items for sale were properly sanitized is unclear.

Leave it in the Dump

One man's trash is another man's treasure—unless you're in the town of Inuvik, Northwest Territories. A 1988 bylaw made it illegal for anyone to dig in and remove garbage from the town dump. The first time you're caught scavenging, you'll have to cough up $50. A second offence will cost you $100. And third and subsequent offences will cost you $300. In the end it's probably cheaper to buy it new! There is, of course, a loophole. The town does make provisions for people to obtain a Solid Waste Salvage Permit.

S'no Easy Job

If you're planning on clearing snow or ice from the sidewalk in front of your home and you live in Saskatoon, Saskatchewan, make sure you don't dump the contents of your shovel on the boulevard. A 1977 bylaw in that community says that's dumping waste contrary to the Anti-Dumping Bylaw, and the offence could cost you as much as $500 in fines.

No Loopholes Here

The anti-litter bylaw in Winnipeg, Manitoba, may have originated several years ago, but the city still takes the issue of litter seriously. In 2002, the council updated the city's anti-litter bylaw—and the definition of what constitutes litter is pretty all encompassing. As stated in the bylaw, litter "means animal and agricultural wastes, ashes, construction and demolition wastes, dead animals, garbage, industrial refuse, rubbish, solid wastes or refuse, abandoned or unattended shopping carts and special wastes, including but not limited to street cleanings, containers, packages, bottles, cans or parts thereof and any deserted or discarded article, product or goods of manufacture." And anyone carelessly disposing of any of these items, on public or even private property, will face the wrath of the bylaw officer.

Tragedy Strikes

The city of Windsor, Ontario, enacted a bylaw in 1953 stating that anyone discarding a refrigerator, freezer or other similar container must remove the doors. The need for this law emerged when two young children suffocated after they were unable to escape from the refrigerator they were playing in.

Don't Paint that Ladder

It's been said that painting a ladder is against the law in Wawa, Ontario. It's true! Occupational Safety and Administration states: "Wood ladders must not be coated with any opaque covering...." That's because paint can hide defects in ladder construction leading to unsafe use of said ladder. Huh? Who knew?

AN ORDERLY FASHION

Your Number Is Up

According to the most recent count, the town of Morden, Manitoba, is a community of about 6200 people. And yet it appears that prior to 2004, a considerable number of homes and buildings on "streets, roads or other thoroughfares" in town didn't have street numbers affixed to the front of the property. That's when Morden town council enacted a bylaw making it mandatory for property owners to do so. And they had to do it right, too. Numbers had to be a minimum of 4 inches (10 centimetres) in height and "clearly visible from the public street."

The town of Neepawa had a few additional requirements in a similar 2004 bylaw. A house number there has to be a minimum of 5 inches (12.5 centimetres) in height and has to be in a "contrasting colour to the building, house or structure to which it is affixed."

Publishing Practices

It is law in Newfoundland that book publishers provide three bound copies of newly published books to the government within one month of being printed. One copy goes to the Department of Municipal and Provincial Affairs, and the other two copies are placed in a library or other location as directed by the Lieutenant-Governor in Council.

Everywhere a Sign

Who knew regulating signs in your community could be so cumbersome? The district of Chetwynd, BC, takes the legalities around signs so seriously that in June 1996 they produced a 22-page bylaw documenting all the requirements to obtain a permit before a sign can be legally erected. Here are just a few of the highlights—the abridged version, of course:

- ☛ Aside from explaining what exactly constitutes a "sign," the bylaw goes on to define 21 different possible types of signs ranging from real estate signs and sandwich boards to illuminated, political, portable, fascia, directional, canopy and changeable copy signs, among others.

- ☛ When erecting your sign, you'd better have a clear understanding of the rules about its appearance, the allowable size, how far your sign can project from the outside wall of the building to which it may be attached and where you're permitted to place it, to name just a few restrictions. The bylaw provides minute details for every sign type.

- ☛ Disposing of redundant signs is also regulated.

- ☛ Oh, and one more thing. You may have a reprieve from following the rules after all. The bylaw doesn't apply to signs or "notices" issued by a provincial body, traffic control devices, vehicle signs or "signs located in the interior of buildings and not visible from a highway." Imagine that!

Of course, permits cost money. In Chetwynd, the permit fee for erecting a sign is complicated and depends on the "value of the sign and any supporting structure."

Just a few months after enacting the sign bylaw, the district of Chetwynd made one change to their initial rules by increasing the amount of liability insurance required to put up a sign from a minimum of $1000 to $2000.

While larger cities often have similar sign bylaws, for a small community like Chetwynd, this bylaw is unique indeed!

A Thundering World Wonder

A protected site it may be, but that hasn't stopped daredevils from around the world from tackling the thundering force of Niagara Falls. Common sense aside, the Niagara Parks Act is quite explicit about what visitors can and cannot do while visiting the park, especially when it comes to the falls itself.

Throughout history, a few adventurers have tried barrelling over the falls—quite literally—and lived to tell the tale. In fact, the attempts occurred often enough that officials decided to create a law forbidding any such stunts without written permission.

And if you're organizing a visit to this wonder of the world, you also shouldn't plan on playing an instrument of any kind, flying a flag, organizing a marching band or "performing any other act that congregates or is likely to congregate persons" without making arrangements first. You need written permission to do any of these activities as well.

For the Common Good

The city of Halifax, Nova Scotia, is mighty proud of its parklands. But one area, a park called the Commons, has special significance. In 1940, the city passed special bylaws to protect the area. Most are logical—no driving on the grass, no damaging the shrubs and trees. But when reading others, you can't help but wonder what may have happened to incite council to "spell it out," as it were. Apparently, it is illegal to dump a dead animal in the Commons, and don't even think about driving your herd of cattle through the area. Both offences could cost you $20 or 10 days in jail.

HOT BUTTON ISSUES

Squelch That Fire Pit!

Roasted weenies fresh from the fire are against the law in the city of Grande Prairie, Alberta. In 1989 the city enacted a bylaw to "prohibit open burning within the corporate limits of the city of Grande Prairie." Of course, a prohibition of any kind usually has its loopholes. In this situation, if you have an extreme case of the open-fire munchies, all you have to do is build a receptacle for the purpose, get permission from the landowner (if that's not you) and pay the city for a fire permit.

An Explosive Situation

Business owners in the municipality of Jasper, Alberta, cannot "possess, store, use, sell or offer for sale any explosive." Now, if you need to blast your way through a mountainside, you can apply to the town council for an explosives permit. But if you are granted your request, you'll still have to go elsewhere to buy the dangerous goods.

The Bell Tolls for All

While town fathers in Peace River, Alberta, didn't enact a bylaw on tolling the town bell, they did pass a motion in 1920 requiring the town constable to "toll the fire bell one stroke for every hour at 8:00 AM, 12:00 noon and 6:00 PM." While the practice is no longer followed to the letter, the motion is still on the books, and today, a bell still rings out every weekday at noon.

Banned, Banned, Banned!

That's all there is to say—in October 2005, the city of White Rock, BC, banned all sales, disposal, ignition and discharge of fireworks within city limits. People wanting to celebrate a special event can apply for a special permit, but they still have to travel to acquire the banned goods!

SHHH!

Censorship

The Censoring of Moving Pictures Act, passed in 1970, can still be found in the 1990 Revised Statues of Newfoundland. According to that law, "a quorum of the members of the board of censors present at an exhibition may, by oral or written notification to the proprietor of that exhibition or to the person operating the projection machine at the exhibition, summarily prohibit the exhibition of a moving or stationary picture, film or slide which they consider to be injurious to the morals of the public, or against the public welfare, or offensive to the public." Interestingly enough, adult videos are available from stores even in Newfoundland.

Music Mania

Perhaps it was a case of excessive musical gatherings popping up here and there without warning. Whatever the reason, in 1981, Grande Prairie made it illegal for any outdoor festival to strike its first chord without acquiring a permit. In fact, aspiring music festival organizers have to apply for the permit a minimum of 60 days in advance of a planned event.

Silence Please!

At the turn of the 20th century, Nova Scotia made it illegal for any on-duty policeman to utter a single word, phrase or sentence to the public. The only exception was if he was speaking in an official capacity.

Policemen had to be above reproach in their personal lives as well. In 1891, a policeman in Yarmouth, Nova Scotia, who was caught drunk, visiting a liquor store or gambling house (unless doing so in the execution of his duties) or using "ungentlemanly language" would be "immediately dismissed from the service." He could also face charges and fines.

EAT, DRINK,
AND BE LEGISLATED

Real Butter

If you go by colour alone, there is no way you can mistake margarine for butter in Québec. That's because the vegetable-based spread can't contain more than "one and six-tenths degrees or less than 10 and five-tenths degrees of yellow or yellow and red combined on the Lovibond colorimeter scale." In layman's terms, that means the colour of margarine can't come anywhere close to that of butter.

What's the Buzz?

It is illegal for clear sodas to contain caffeine in Canada.

Information Mandate
The city council of White Rock, BC, enacted a bylaw in 1994 making it law for any business selling liquor to post signs in prominent locations warning women of the dangers of drinking during pregnancy. To send a consistent message throughout the community, all liquor outlets had to post the same warning.

THINK GLOBALLY, ACT LOCALLY

No Nukes!

Out of great concern for the safety of their citizens and the citizens of the world, the town of Fort Saskatchewan, Alberta, enacted a bylaw in 1983 stating a referendum on nuclear disarmament would be held in conjunction with municipal elections that year. While the referendum did indeed occur, the only record of any follow-up was a letter forwarded by the council of the day to the member of Parliament for that area "expressing council's concern regarding nuclear arms and asking the MP to bring to the federal government a referendum in the next federal election." Though council received a response to that request, there is no mention in the meeting minutes of what the reply was.

Check This Out!

The powers that be in Chilliwack, BC, recently enacted a bylaw that might be the first of its kind in Canada. On January 23, 2006, council members in that city passed the Hydroponics and Drug Paraphernalia Bylaw 2006. Simply put, anyone dealing in drug paraphernalia or in substances that in large batches could be used for narcotic production must be identified and potentially monitored under this act. Anyone selling drug paraphernalia has to register the following:

- the "name, residence, or street address and birth date of the buyer,"
- picture identification,
- a description of the item purchased,
- the price paid, and
- the date of purchase.

So, basically speaking, the RCMP will know of the sale of every item that could potentially have any association with drugs and drug production, along with the name and contact information of the purchaser. Yup, there's nowhere to hide in Chilliwack!

Don't Even Try It

Torture is against the law in the Yukon, no matter whether you are a public official or not. The 2002 Revised Statutes of the Yukon officially upheld the United Nations Convention Against Torture and Other Cruel, Inhuman or Degrading Treatment or Punishment. In the statute, torture means any kind of physical, mental or emotional pain inflicted on a person to elicit a statement or information.

CAUSE FOR A CELEBRATION

Happy Holidays

Most bylaws were established to provide restrictions of some sort, and if you broke those restrictions, you broke the law. But in 1959, in Williams Lake, BC, the village commission passed a happy law making January 2 an official holiday. The name of that holiday? Wrestling Day.

The origins of the holiday come from two pioneer merchants, Alistair Mackenzie and Syd Western. Legend has it the two shopkeepers were having coffee one January 2 some time in the 1930s. It was cold. The streets were empty. No one had come into their respective businesses all morning. And after talking to a few of other business owners on the town's main drag, they decided to close shop for the day. After all, the day after Christmas was a holiday. It seemed only reasonable that the day after New Year's would be a holiday as well. In 1943, the town declared January 2 a holiday, but it wasn't made law until 1959. The story goes that the holiday earned the name Wrestling Day because "half the town was wrestling with a hangover."

In 1976, all existing store-closing bylaws were abolished, including Wrestling Day. That put the town in an uproar, and after much public pressure, council reinstated the Wrestling Day bylaw the following year. It remains in effect to this day.

That's the Spirit!

While Boxing Day is a holiday we all take for granted, it evolved from community to community throughout the British Commonwealth at different times over the years. Here in Canada, the city of Windsor, Ontario, passed a law in 1937, making the day following Christmas a holiday. Council justified this law by stating it was "for the health, safety, morality and welfare of the inhabitants of the municipality." But when the law was forwarded for approval to Ontario's Department of Municipal Affairs, it was returned unapproved. It was the opinion of the supervisor at the time that "the municipality has no power to fix such a public holiday." Two years later, the issue was raised again. Council proposed the day following Christmas would be a civic holiday called Boxing Day. The bylaw was passed and became law on December 19, 1939.

A Golden Celebration

Everyone loves a holiday, and councillors in Bowden, Alberta, decided that bestowing a day of rest on their residents was the best way to celebrate the province's Golden Jubilee. So for one day, August 17, 1955, a civic holiday was proclaimed to "augment the importance of the Alberta Golden Jubilee and the success of the Gigantic Community picnic."

Heritage Celebrations

Citizens of the Yukon are encouraged to "reflect on the history and heritage of their land and its peoples" on June 13 of every year after their Legislative Assembly passed the Yukon Day Act in 1998. The date was chosen because it was the anniversary of "the creation of Yukon as a territory within Canada" 100 years earlier.

Any Excuse for a Party

It doesn't take long to think up a reason for a holiday—or a festival. For folks in the town of Collingwood, Ontario, celebrating all things Elvis is reason enough. The annual four-day celebration is anticipated by residents and visitors alike. Although the town council hasn't deemed the King of Rock 'n' Roll worthy of a four-day vacation from work, they did pass a bylaw outlining rules and responsibilities for the Collingwood Elvis Festival Board in 2001.

ENVIRONMENT FRIENDLY

Tree Hugging at Its Finest

You can cut trees in the district of Hope, BC. Well, sometimes you can. That community's 1995 tree protection bylaw makes it clear that anyone who wants to cut down a tree must get a permit first. However, you'll only get a permit if your request follows some specific regulations. Among other things, you have to provide the city's municipal engineer with a letter explaining why you need to cut the tree, a tree survey and proof of liability insurance carried by the tree-removal company being used for the job.

Water Rations

In 1915, residents of the town of Cochrane, Alberta, were able to access drinking water from street taps—but not without paying for the privilege first. Using town water cost residents 75 cents every three months, and the fee had to be paid in advance. A midnight visit to the town's water source didn't mean you'd get off without paying. If you were caught, it could cost you $25—a whole lot more than the initial 75 cents.

I'm Even, You're Odd

The district of Hope, BC, deals with water conservation differently. In that community, water rationing isn't just a weather-related situation whereby residents are called to observe certain rules because of a drought. Since June 2005, homeowners there have been restricted to watering their lawns on even or odd days, depending on their particular street address, from May 1 to September 30 of every year. The penalty for getting your days mixed up is $100 a day and could increase to a maximum fine of $2000, depending on how long you continue the unlawful behaviour.

The municipality of Crowsnest Pass, BC, adds yet another twist to its watering rules. Council there passed a bylaw in 2004 restricting people with even house numbers to water their lawns on Tuesdays, Thursdays and Saturdays between 6:00 AM and 9:00 AM or 7:00 PM and 11:00 PM. Those with odd house numbers have Wednesdays, Fridays and Sundays to water their lawns. And "there shall be NO outside watering on Monday."

Water, Water, Nowhere...

In 1927, the watering of lawns and gardens in the town of Wilkie, Saskatchewan, was strictly regulated. A bylaw stipulated that watering with a hose could only occur between 6:00 PM and 10:00 PM from June to August. Break the law once and you could face a $50 fine or 30 days in jail. Break it twice in the same season, and the town could disconnect water services to your home for the remainder of that summer.

WILD TIMES

No Closed Doors Here

Using an escort service might seem a bit daring to most folk, but the city of Medicine Hat, Alberta, decided demystifying the situation was the best way to keep it on the up and up—and they did just that by enacting a bylaw to "regulate escorts and agencies." Before anyone can hang a shingle advertising escort services, he or she must obtain a licence from the city. Each licence issued includes the individual's full name, including all given names, their birthday and home address, telephone number, the agency they work for, any aliases and a current photograph. Get caught doing business without a licence, and the fine is anywhere between $500 and $1500 each time.

Age of Majority?

A 1958 bylaw that is still in effect today prohibits youth under age 18 years to "be or remain in a poolroom, or to play pool or any other game" inside a pool hall in White Rock, BC. Underage youth can't work there either—and anyone who does work there won't be clocking out any later than 11:30 PM. That's when all poolrooms must be closed for business.

LOCK 'EM UP

Jail Bait

It didn't matter how sorry you felt for your buddy who found himself locked up in the town clink. As of May 17, 1883, it was no longer legal in the town of Orillia, Ontario, for you to pass a flask of whiskey through the jail bars on your daily visit. Likely, inebriated prisoners were far more difficult to control than sober ones.

Twenty-five Stripes

From misdemeanours to felony charges or murder, criminals of all sorts in Newfoundland could face whipping and hard labour while serving time in jail in 1892. Each time a prisoner stepped out of line, the jail guard could privately or publicly issue three lashes "provided that not more than 25 stripes shall be given at any one time."

UNDERWATER

Out of Sight, Not Necessarily Out of Mind

Submarine telegraph cables in Newfoundland were protected like an endangered species. According to the Newfoundland Act of 1892, anyone breaking or damaging a submarine cable in any way could be subject to a prison term of three months or a fine of $500. Exactly how an ordinary Joe could manage the deep-sea vandalism is beyond imagining.

Pristine Waters

No one can cast stones—or ballast or anything else for that matter—into St. John's harbour in Newfoundland. Try it and you could face a $50 fine or 50 days in jail.

Fact or Fiction?

While I was researching this collection of unique laws in this fine country of ours, a number of well-intentioned individuals provided interesting tidbits they admitted they were unable to confirm. Some were so wonderfully bizarre that I simply couldn't help but include them in this section.

Should you, dear reader, have any inside information on one or more of these bylaws or know of a unique law or two I didn't include, please don't hesitate call. Who knows, maybe there's a volume two in the making?

BUT IS IT A LAW?

- Rumour has it that a bylaw in the town of Yarmouth, Nova Scotia, regulated the length of women's skirts until the 1960s.
- At least one curfew bylaw in Canada had a rather odd twist to it. Apparently, in the town of Yarmouth, Nova Scotia, African Canadians were not allowed in certain areas of town at night.
- It is illegal to drive your cows across Water Street in St. John's, Newfoundland, before 11:00 AM on Sundays—or is it?
- Exercise might be good for your health, but if your efforts at longevity frighten a horse in Quesnel, BC, then you could be in trouble—or so the story goes.
- It really is against the law to display advertisements in English in the province of Québec. On the other hand, it is rumoured that a Montréal bylaw states you cannot swear in French.
- Apparently, at one time in the province of Alberta, a newly released prisoner was provided with a handgun, bullets and a horse so he could safely ride out of town.
- Showing public affection on a Sunday in Wawa, Ontario, was supposedly against the law at one time.
- Maybe it's for the comfort of the cow, or the sensory well being of its caregivers, but according to one urban legend, it's against the law to keep a cow in your house in St. John's, Newfoundland. Rumour also has it that running cattle through city streets in St. John's has to happen before 8:00 AM, or you'll face a fine.
- Legend has it that the city of Toronto, Ontario, has had a few strange laws on the books at one time or another. Apparently, dragging a dead horse down Yonge Street on a Sunday was illegal. And riding a streetcar on a Sunday after eating garlic could also get you into trouble. A review of current bylaws seems to indicate these bylaws have been repealed—or were they ever in existence?

- ☞ In Canada, it is against the law to remove a bandage in public—or so some say.
- ☞ Allowing your dog to bark, especially during the night, is likely a no-no in many communities, but who ever heard of keeping your parrot quiet? One source suggests a $100 fine is laid against people in Oak Bay, BC, if they have noisy pet parrots.
- ☞ Apparently, it is (or was at one time) against the law to kill a sasquatch in British Columbia. Though the creature's existence has yet to be proven, should the sasquatch be anything more than a legend, it seems logical that killing one wouldn't be such a great idea.

- ☞ You can't depend on a roll of the dice while playing craps in Alberta.
- ☞ Rumour has it that cats older than six months had to be spayed or neutered in Port Coquitlam, BC, unless a special breeding permit was purchased from the city. It may have been a law in the past, but it's not currently on the books.

☛ Newly laundered clothes with that fresh-from-the-clothesline scent aren't possible in Kanata, Ontario. Apparently, it is illegal there to have a clothesline in one's backyard.

☛ At one time, a city bylaw restricted the colour of one's house and garage door in Kanata, Ontario. Beaconsfield, Ontario, apparently had a bylaw on books stating residents could not have more than two different colours of exterior paint on their homes. And in Outremont, Québec, exterior paint jobs weren't the only home improvement issue up for discussion. Apparently, in one case, the city of Outremont went to the Appeals Court over the type of division allowed inside a window frame.

☛ Youngsters have had their zest for adventure curbed slightly in Oshawa, Ontario. Supposedly, it is against the law for anyone to climb trees in that city.

☛ In Etobicoke, Ontario, bubble baths are likely a rarity since rumour has it that a bylaw states residents there can't have more than 3.5 inches (9 centimetres) of water in the bathtub.

☛ Theatre owners have to pay attention to the clock in Montréal, Québec. Apparently in that city it is illegal for a movie playing in the theatre to end later than 2:00 AM.

☛ If you like wandering about in your birthday suit and live in Winnipeg, Manitoba, you'd better make sure you have your blinds down and drapes drawn. If not, you could be breaking a city bylaw.

☛ Meeting the woman of your dreams wasn't possible for the men of Edmonton, Alberta, at least not if they were tossing a few back at their neighbourhood pub after work. One unconfirmed source suggests it was once illegal for a "man to drink with a woman in an Edmonton beer parlour."

☛ While the current existence of the British Columbia Grasshopper Control Committee has yet to be confirmed, it's said to be against the law to interrupt one of their meetings. Anyone doing so could be arrested.

- Wearing a bathing suit while "loitering, playing or indulging in a sun bath in any park or on the beach" was supposedly illegal in Victoria, BC.
- One source, apparently drawing their information from the provincial law books, stated it was once illegal to watch exotic dancers while drinking alcohol in Saskatchewan.
- A city ordinance in Churchill, Manitoba, states children there aren't allowed to wear furry costumes while trick or treating during Halloween. Apparently the concern is they could be mistaken for an animal, and in particular for a baby seal, and inadvertently attract polar bears to town.
- There's no excuse for sloppy dress in Fort Qu'Appelle, Saskatchewan. It's said to be against the law for teens to walk down Main Street with their shoes untied.
- It is—or was at one time—against the law in Ottawa, Ontario, for children to eat ice cream cones on city streets on Sunday.
- Public property must be treated with respect in Winnipeg, Manitoba. One source states a bylaw in that city makes it illegal for pedestrians to strike sidewalks with a metal object.
- Pigs weren't made for wandering. One source suggested pigs wandering the streets of Toronto, Ontario, in 1934 were in deep trouble.
- You'd think it would be considered fair play, but one unconfirmed source states it's illegal to try and catch a fish with your hands in Saskatoon, Saskatchewan.
- The information highway has a predetermined speed limit in Uxbridge, Ontario. Apparently, residents there can't have an Internet connection faster than 56K.
- In Canada, you cannot pay for a 50-cent item with 50 pennies.
- If you find yourself bankrupt, and you have a predisposition to excessive alcohol consumption, one source points to BC as the best place in Canada to get locked up. That's because jailers there are supposedly required to "bring convicted debtors a pint of beer on demand."

☞ While you can purchase individual cans of beer in some Canadian provinces, it's apparently the law in Newfoundland and New Brunswick that the smallest unit of beer that can be sold in liquor stores is a six-pack.

Definitely Legend

*It's interesting how some sources cite chapter and verse,
and yet their claims are not easily verified.*

*While the following entry was said to be true, no date was
offered, and as of 2005, the citation was erroneous.*

THE LAW THAT WASN'T

Don't Ruffle My Feathers

An Internet site claims section 331 of the Canadian Criminal Code makes it "illegal to send a letter or telegram threatening a bird." The Criminal Code of any country is ever evolving, and today the section stated refers to "theft by person holding power of attorney." Whether the claimed law ever existed is doubtful.

No Such Law...Not Yet

On its way to legislation, a proposed law goes
through a number of twists and turns and sometimes
unorthodox processes.

Here are just a couple of hotly debated laws that can't
help but evoke a response of some type.

SPICING THINGS UP...
AT LEAST ONCE
A YEAR

No Headaches Allowed

Leave it to the imagination of one of Canada's quirky authors to come up with an idea for a proclamation that could blow the roof off the fallacy that we Canadians are an uptight, sexually stunted lot. According to a 2004 article by *Toronto Sun* columnist Valerie Gibson, Chris Gudgeon, best-selling author of *The Naked Truth: The Untold Story of Sex in Canada*, suggested May 14 be declared National Sex Day. His chosen date was significant because it was the anniversary of the day Pierre Trudeau's government passed the Omnibus Bill, which addressed previously taboo topics including abortion and birth control.

Gudgeon wasn't alone in his quest. Sue McGarvie, therapist and *Sex with Sue* radio host, and Valerie Scott, spokesperson for Sex Professionals of Canada, added their voices to the cause. McGarvie was quoted as saying it would be a "fun" idea. "Sex is, after all, good for you!...Maybe everyone could spend the day in bed on National Sex Day?"

WATER, WATER, EVERYWHERE

Ancient Innovations

While it's not yet law in the town of Cochrane, Alberta, council members there has put their muscle behind a not-so-new idea they hope will take off. Running with the motto "You don't know the value of water until the well is running dry," residents in the western town are being encouraged to harvest rain in a rain barrel. After all, it takes no real effort, and it's such a shame to waste all that "free and pure rain water." They're even encouraging residents to consider attaching a hose to their barrel to make for "more practical, 'hands-free' watering." The hope is to reduce the amount of treated water used in lawn and garden care. Whether this actually becomes a bylaw is yet to be seen.

WHERE THERE'S SMOKE...

The Great Marijuana Debate

Marijuana was once clearly against the law, and those who flirted with Mary Jane were thought of by most Canadians as not the kind of people mother would like you to bring home for dinner. But legalizing pot has developed into one of Canada's judicial system's hottest topics of debate.

In 1923, marijuana was banned in Canada under the Opium and Drug Act. While the 1960s were a time of free love and experimentation of all sorts, it wasn't until the 21st century that Canada started seriously reviewing its stand on the matter. Was marijuana really a dangerous drug?

In a 2003 report, *Decriminalization of Marijuana in Canada*, then–Justice Minister Martin Cauchon was quoted as saying Canadian laws on the topic needed some updating.

The previous year, a special Senate committee on illegal drugs suggested marijuana be treated like tobacco or alcohol. The House of Commons was wading through intricate studies on whether marijuana was a gateway drug, how it affected users and if it was really prudent to saddle an otherwise-productive individual with a criminal record because he was found to have a joint or two in his possession. While those supporting decriminalization were hopeful that what they believed to be a strange and antiquated law would be modernized, others looked at Canada and wondered if our leaders had lost their minds. Interestingly enough, the proposed Act to Amend the Contraventions Act and the Controlled Drugs and Substances Act, originally tabled in May of 2003, died on the order paper once the 2004 election was called.

No matter what side of the fence you stand on, the situation is likely as weird, strange and odd as any other law in this collection. But regardless your view, possession of marijuana is still against the law in Canada.

THE PUBLIC EYE

Big Brother is Watching

Don't say that—someone might be listening! In November 2005, the House of Commons reviewed a proposed law that, if passed, would have allowed police and other officials to get personal information about people of interest to national security. If passed, telephone and Internet providers would have been required to "phase out technical barriers to police and security agencies seeking access to messages or conversations." The goal was to restrict communication between "terrorists and other criminals" and also prevent a child pornographer, for example, from "sending his disgusting images around this country and around the world," explained then–Public Safety Minister Anne McLellan in a statement to the Canadian Press.

Advocates for privacy rights argued it was against the Canadian Charter of Rights and Freedoms to do such a thing, and telephone and internet providers raised practical concerns about new equipment needed to preserve electronic data and the costs incurred by working with security agencies.

Although the law was introduced into the House, like the great marijuana debate, it too died on the order paper with the early January call of the 2006 election.

ABOUT THE AUTHOR

Lisa Wojna

Lisa Wojna, author of two other non-fiction books, has worked in the community newspaper industry as a writer and journalist and has travelled all over Canada, from the windy prairies of Manitoba to northern British Columbia, and even to the wilds of Africa. Although writing and photography have been a central part of her life for as long as she can remember, it's the people behind every story that are her motivation and give her the most fulfillment.

ABOUT THE ILLUSTRATOR

Roger Garcia

Roger Garcia immigrated to Canada from El Salvador at the age of seven. Because of the language barrier, he had to find a way to communicate with other kids. That's when he discovered the art of tracing. It wasn't long before he mastered this highly skilled technique, and by age 14, he was drawing weekly cartoons for the *Edmonton Examiner*. He taught himself to paint and sculpt, and then in high school and college, Roger skipped class to hide in the art room all day in order to further explore his talent. Currently, Roger's work can be seen in a local weekly newspaper and in places around Edmonton.